Interactive
Computer
Graphics

Computer Systems Engineering Series

Douglas Lewin, *Editor*

◆

Computer Interfacing and On-Line Operation
J. C. Cluley

Interactive Computer Graphics
B. S. Walker, J. R. Gurd *and* E. A. Drawneek

Automata Theory: An Engineering Approach
Igor Aleksander *and* F. Keith Hanna

computer systems engineering series

Interactive Computer Graphics

B. S. Walker

J. R. Gurd

E. A. Drawneek

Crane Russak • New York

Edward Arnold • London

Interactive Computer Graphics

Published in the United States by

Crane, Russak & Company, Inc.
347 Madison Avenue
New York, N.Y. 10017

First published in Great Britain in 1976 by

Edward Arnold (Publishers) Ltd.
25 Hill Street
London, W1X 8LL

Crane, Russak ISBN 0-8448-0650-1
Edward Arnold ISBN 0-7131-2505-5

LC 74-24985

Printed in the United States of America

Contents

Editor's Foreword

The continuing expansion of knowledge in the computer sciences means that it is now more important than ever for the professional computer engineer to keep abreast of the latest developments in his field. Moreover, due to the rapid assimilation of computer techniques into all areas of science and engineering, non-specialists are also finding it essential to acquire expertise in these disciplines. Thus, there exists a need for readable, up-to-date texts on relevant specialist topics of computer engineering which can form authoritative source books for both the practicing engineer and the academic.

This series is an attempt to fulfill such a requirement and is directed primarily at the professional engineer and graduate student in computer technology; in many cases the books will also meet the needs of specialist options offered in undergraduate courses.

The texts will embrace all aspects of computer systems design with an overall emphasis on the engineering of integrated hardware–software systems. In general the series will present established theory and techniques which have found direct application in systems design. However, promising new theoretical methods will also be covered.

All the books will follow a similar basic pattern of a review of the fundamental aspects of the subject, followed by a survey of the current state of the art, and, where applicable, design examples. An important feature will be the associated bibliography and references, which will select the more important and fundamental publications. The objective is to bring the reader up to a level in the subject where he can read current technical papers and apply the results to his own research and design activities. In the main, authors will be chosen from specialists in their field, drawn from both industrial and academic environments, and experienced in communicating technical ideas.

New books will be regularly added to the series to provide an up-to-date source of specialist texts in Computer Systems Engineering.

DOUGLAS LEWIN
Brunel University

vii

Preface

The major part of this book was written during the spring and early summer of 1974. Inevitably some changes in the status of interactive computer graphics have already taken place. By and large, however, the techniques described in the book are still in wide use. Most effort is now being invested in developing applications. It is to be hoped that new techniques and uses continue to be found for this natural form of man/computer interaction.

The authors would like to make the following grateful acknowledgments for the help they have received in preparing the manuscript:

To Mrs. J. Wild, Mrs. R. Drawneek and Mrs. E. Atkinson for typing the manuscripts

To Mr. P. Clegg for drawing such a complex set of diagrams

To Mr. P. Atkinson and Mr. J. Patterson for their cooperation in describing their applications and providing Figures 1.1 and 1.4

To CASE Ltd., for providing Figure 2.8

To REDAC Ltd., for their interest and information on their programs, together with Figures 1.2 and 1.3

To DEC Ltd., for their assistance and information on the GT40 system.

Mr. Walker wrote the basis of Chapters 1 and 2, Dr. Drawneek wrote that of Chapter 3, and Mr. Gurd that of Chapter 4.

The three different resulting linguistic styles were to some extent homogenized by Mr. Gurd when editing together the whole work. The authors hope that the end result will be as enjoyable to read as it was to produce.

B.S.W.

J.R.G.

E.A.D.

Interactive Computer Graphics as an Aid to Man-Computer Communication

1.1. INTRODUCTION

The Background

Over the past century, mechanization has vastly enhanced man's physical capability; the computer offers a commensurate enhancement to his mental capability, but it is a recently developed tool and we have yet to grasp the full opportunity it offers. One direction in which development is vital is towards satisfactory human communication with the computer. The telegram may be adequate as a means of conveying greetings or laying bets, but it is not adequate for communication with, for example, a mathematics tutor or a financial adviser. Yet it remains our standard means of communication with our computer.

The time is coming when we shall talk with computers, but, even when we can do this easily, speech communication alone is not adequate for many purposes. The human uses his eyes to take in information and there are many things that it is easier to draw than say. Vocal communication with computers may be not far off, but there is still a lot of research and development to be accomplished before it can become a useful reality. This is not the case with visual communication. The technology for this exists now; quite sophisticated systems have been designed and built, though at a cost that makes them uneconomical for many users, and simply not available to most. As yet, regrettably, few people have developed simple cheap systems, but the feasibility of such systems has been explored, and it, too, does exist. Interactive computer graphics, the technique of visual communication between man and computer, is a practicable and simple reality, and can be readily achieved.

The first important manifestation of computer graphics was at MIT in 1963, when SKETCHPAD was demonstrated (1). In this demonstration a cathode-ray oscilloscope was driven by the Lincoln TX2 computer in such a way that it generated geometrical figures. Using a device called a light pen, the figures on the screen could be drawn and manipulated. It was an impressive demonstration and, seen for the first time, seemed almost magical. With hindsight, it is important to realize that it was only a demonstration of the possibilities of the technique. The useful work the program could do was little. The system was expensive because the computer used was a very powerful one judged against the standards of the time, yet driving the display posed a heavy load on it. It generated on the screen images that any child could draw with a school geometry set. Nevertheless it was important; it showed the way to a breakthrough in man–machine communication, to the possibility of interacting with a computer other than by telegram.

Soon after SKETCHPAD, various computer manufacturers realized the possibility of a demand for computer graphics, and laid on their designers and engineers the task of producing equipment and systems for the market. It became almost obligatory to have computer graphics units, at least in the catalog. They were expensive, but some were made and sold, and these paved the way for the sophisticated systems now in use in the aircraft industry and similar fields where they can be shown to be cost effective, and where large sums of money are available for research and development. Unfortunately, because of the cost, the expected universal adoption of interactive computer graphics did not materialize.

There was, however, one area of growth, that of the *visual display unit* or *VDU*, which is now readily available and widely used. These units usually make use of a cathode-ray oscilloscope as a computer output device, but they are restricted to various types of fixed-format alphanumeric display. They are available at costs of the same order as teletypes. They produce much the same limited range of output as teletypes, but they are quiet, do not generate waste paper, and are in other ways convenient to use. They do not escape from the restriction of communication by telegram.

The technical reasons why interactive systems capable of geometrical displays have stayed so costly will be brought out later in this book; there are also reasons which are circumstantial. The field of computer development and manufacture has always been highly competitive. Its advances have been swift, almost headlong, and many have found this to their cost. Hard-pressed designers and engineers have had little opportunity to stop and think, or to restart from first principles. Systems, like Topsy in the story book, have "just growed and growed".

Some users had tasks particularly amenable to graphics, and had the vision and the resources to make use of the new technique. For these users the hardware cost of a few terminals was not significant, especially when compared with their overall computing costs. In this case there was not much pressure on manufacturers to be economical in their designs. It was profitable to try and produce all things for some men, but less so to try and produce some things for all men. Thus few simple, cheap systems were made available. Even the few systems which were marketed in this category had a surprisingly limited success; there is a circumstantial reason for this, also.

This new form of man–machine interaction is analogous to a new form of language of which nobody has any prior experience. A lot of preliminary work must be done in each and every problem area before the means is sufficiently sophisticated to have effective practical application. Virtually everybody who sits at a computer-graphics console has to start from scratch, as did the first computer users and programmers nearly thirty years ago. It is a privileged few who can afford to do this, because computer power is still expensive, and even the simpler, cheaper computer-graphics systems are only cheap in comparison with other computing costs. In any case many cheap systems are unable to provide interaction because of low transmission rates and the lack of selective erasure. Computing power per unit cost has been much increased over the past decade; paradoxically, this makes the demand for cheapness of graphics equipment even more compelling. An extra thousand dollars or pounds added to the price of a large system, costing millions, does not seem significant. Whereas the MIT machine drove one display in the SKETCHPAD demonstration, the more powerful modern machines may drive tens or even hundreds. Any significant extra cost on the price of one terminal can become multiplied to an amount comparable with the overall system cost.

It may seem strange that the subject of cost has been stressed so much but it is proper that it should. The technologist/designer/engineer is constrained to work within natural laws of a particular kind according to his discipline. He is also constrained by a universal law, whatever his discipline, that of cost and cost effectiveness. To design or engineer without this constraint always in mind is just as disastrous as to overlook the laws of nature.

In summary, the field of interactive computer graphics today is largely unexplored. There are some highly developed systems and sophisticated applications, but they are few. There are a great number of naive systems that are little more than electronic teletypes. In the middle is a large gap that has been sparsely covered, and there is room for a great deal of useful development by many people in the areas of both hardware and software.

Interactive Graphics

Computer graphics means images generated by a computer. Interactive computer graphics means that the human must be involved with the computer through these images. The human must communicate with the computer. Now, the computer can generate images and the human can see them because he has eyes. The human can also generate images, but the computer has no eyes. It cannot therefore take in information in the same way as the human. Information has usually been transferred into computers through keyboards, since in this way the human can generate patterns of pulses which are not far different from the kind of patterns of pulses with which the computer performs its internal operations. A human with a keyboard can generate patterns which are "intelligible" to the computer, i.e. which the computer can process. If interactive computer graphics is to be possible, the terminal, or system which implements it, must work through these same constraints. Before going into details about the nature of the devices and systems which implement computer graphics it is profitable to study some actual working systems. These illustrate *what* has to be done, and lend point to the later descriptions of *how* it is done.

1.2. ILLUSTRATIVE APPLICATIONS OF INTERACTIVE COMPUTER GRAPHICS. A CONTROL ENGINEERING APPLICATION: GRAPH PLOTTING

A commonly used and valuable aid in the design of servo systems and feedback-control systems is known as the Nyquist plot. This is a polar plot producing a locus whose shape gives a control engineer valuable insight into the behavior of a control system, with particular reference to its stability. The plot represents the amplitude and phase of the output with reference to a unit input vector lying on the horizontal positive axis (x axis). The coordinates of the points on the locus are derived from evaluating the *transfer function* of the system over a range of frequencies.

Figure 1.1 shows the Nyquist plot for the transfer function

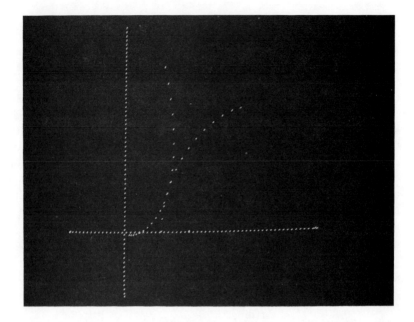

Fig. 1.1 Nyquist plot of the transfer function.

$$H(j\omega) = \frac{10.3(1 + 0.275j\omega)}{j\omega(1 + 0.2j\omega)(1 + 0.05j\omega)(1 + 0.036j\omega)}$$

where ω is the angular frequency in rad/s and $j^2 = -1$. Each point of the locus is found by calculating the polar coordinates (r, θ) as a function of the parameter ω, where

$$r = \frac{10.3}{\omega} \left\{ \frac{1 + (0.275\omega)^2}{[1 + (0.2\omega)^2][1 + (0.05\omega)^2][1 + (0.036\omega)^2]} \right\}^{1/2}$$

and

$$\theta = \tan^{-1}0.275\omega - \tan^{-1}0.2\omega - \tan^{-1}0.05\omega - \tan^{-1}0.036\omega - \pi/2.$$

This is typical of a fairly simple closed-loop control system. In the past a designer would have evaluated the transfer function by slide rule or similar means, and it is easy to see that it was a laborious and tedious process.

Having produced the locus, the designer is particularly concerned with where it crosses the negative x axis, and how near it is to tangential with the calculated circular locus shown, known as an "M-circle". The general shape of the curve and its height above the x axis are also informative. After examining the locus, the designer is normally required to change some of the values of the transfer-function parameters, or to add compensatory terms to the numerator and/or denominator. He then replots the locus, continuing the process until the locus corresponds to the desired behavior.

Using a computer, the transfer function can be entered through the keyboard and the parameter values added. The locus is then presented by the graphics a few seconds later. As each parameter is varied, the curve is redisplayed and the designer makes his alterations in the light of the changing shape of the locus. Finally, using a light pen or similar input device, the designer indicates relevant points on the locus and the computer prints out the coordinates, amplitude, phase, and frequency of the point indicated. Manifestly this process is greatly simplified and speeded up by using a computer. On the other hand, it is essentially an interactive process since the "curve-fitting" aspects are difficult to program, whereas a designer can perform the fitting process easily.

The most important and significant aspect of this example is its simplicity. The plot shown was produced on a simple, cheap "home-made" graphics display; the computer that produced it was a minimal-configuration PDP 8, having only 4096 words of storage. The input-indicating device is a tablet, also "home-made", well within the resources of a college or university department either to buy or to build.

The program described has now been extended to a suite of programs, each of which can be performed by the same minimal-configuration computer. These include system design by the root locus method, and calculating the system's time-domain response using the fast Fourier transform method. These programs, too, are used interactively (2).

This example has been described first, not because it emanates from the authors' own institution, but because it demonstrates how a non-trivial problem can be tackled with limited facilities.

Circuit Design and Component Layout: the REDAC System

This useful and sophisticated system of interactive graphics (REDAC Software Ltd., Tewkesbury, Glos., England) is in use in a number of installations in Europe and America; the Boeing Corporation is notable among US users. Its value will be readily understood by electronic design engineers.

The system consists of a suite of programs which is specifically designed to operate with selected computer-graphics systems. The equipment on which it was developed was an ICL 4130 computer-graphics system (made originally by Elliott Automation). It was then further developed and translated for the DEC PDP 15 general-purpose graphics system. A key aspect of this system is the use of refreshed graphics which provides the all-important instantaneous interaction. Four programs or packages out of the suite are devoted to interactive graphics; some nine more provide facilities, such as error checking and output tape preparation, suitable for numerically controlled drafting machines or for the various special-purpose machines used in printed-circuit-board manufacture.

The three interactive programs deal respectively with the design of integrated circuits, thick/thin-film circuits, and printed-circuit boards. They are all primarily drawing aids aimed at allowing a conventional designer in these fields to exercise his skill to its best effect. This is done by relieving him of much of the routine work of drawing, redrawing, and making trivial calculations. Figure 1.2 illustrates the display unit.

The user, seated before the display, has his field of work displayed to him on a CRT screen. Using a light pen he can build up an image on the screen. The fixed control buttons allow him to control the drawing in a variety of ways. In addition, the program causes the presentation of a "menu" of processes which the user can select by pointing to them with the light pen. The "menu" technique allows flexibility in any system that

Fig. 1.2 Display unit for the REDAC computer-aided circuit design system.

uses it, and is convenient for the user in that he has no problem in identifying or remembering the different functions of the control buttons.

REDAL 1: Integrated-Circuit Design. The nature of the program and drawing process is a direct descendant of the SKETCHPAD system mentioned earlier. It allows the user to draw straight lines and rectangles, and to manipulate or delete them by simple commands. Typical commands are as follows.

DRAW	rectangular shapes
DELETE	items or groups of items
MOVE	items or groups of items
MEASURE	distance between points or lines
EXTEND	any part of a drawn item
NAME	any item or group to store
REPRODUCE	any item or group, named or unnamed

There are two other powerful commands. The first of these is WINDOW. This technique, much used in interactive graphics and described in detail in Chapter 3, allows any part of the whole image to be presented on its own, in magnified form, giving a "zoom lens" effect. The designer can work in fine detail on the magnified section and then revert to an overall view at will. This conforms to a common pattern of mental activity in systems design, as we shall see in Chapter 4. The second command is of particular value in the design of multilayer systems such as monolithic integrated circuits. The program allows the user to deal with up to six layers simultaneously. The command REDEFINE allows different brightness values to be used in the display of each layer so that where they are superimposed they are still distinguishable.

It should be noted that the program contains nothing that is, in itself, particular to integrated circuits. This aspect of the design is entirely exercised by the human user; the machine merely does the drawing for him and the necessary "housekeeping".

REDAL 2: Thick/Thin-Film Circuit Design. This program logically follows on from REDAL 1 and SKETCHPAD; some more of the specialized and repetitive processes are delegated to the machine, allowing the human designer more freedom to exercise his skill without his train of thought being interrupted. The program is based, as before, on lines and rectangles.

In the interconnection of elements in thin- or thick-film circuits the conductor tracks have to be drawn with specified widths. In this program the user specifies the width and indicates the route; the computer draws the track accordingly. Likewise, resistor and capacitor values depend on the areas, lengths, and widths. The user declares the value per unit area of a component, and indicates its position and length with the light pen; the computer continuously computes and displays the width, while maintaining the scale.

When the designer is satisfied with the layout he commands the system to produce a tape from the final image. This tape is suitable for controlling an automatic drafting machine, which in turn produces a master drawing which is ready for photography.

REDAL 3/14: Printed-Circuit-Board (PCB) Design. This program is a further development of the other two, once more depending on the drawing of lines and rectangles. It has added sophistication to take advantage of the standardization of PCB's and electronic components and to help the designer with particular problems of PCB design.

In this program, before the graphics is activated, the computer is fed with the specifications of the components and PCB, which may be a multilayer, single-sided or double-sided board. This information is entered using paper-tape input.

When the graphics is activated, the computer presents an image, with component outlines, connection "pads", and edge-connector pads (if specified). A semi-automatic process is used to derive the first arrangement, depending on the input instructions. The interconnections, also entered with the original input data, are drawn in as straight lines "point to point". The designer commences by replacing the point-to-point lines by routed lines using the light pen. "Plate throughs" and "crossovers" are marked and noted automatically. The automatic routines are called in to help when the designer achieves firstly a placement of components and then a routing pattern. Meanwhile the program checks continuously with the specification for wrong or duplicated connections. At any time the designer can intervene and interactively modify the placement or routing pattern.

The question naturally arises as to why the interconnections cannot be drawn automatically, without the aid of the designer. Programs which attempt this have been written but, in general, human intervention has been shown to be necessary; the human intelligence seems to grasp complex topological problems in a way that the programmed computer cannot. Furthermore, the designer usually has the capability and authority to manipulate the specification. For instance, the number of crossovers and plate throughs must normally be reduced to a minimum. The designer knows the minimum and can assess the consequences of relaxing the stringency of the imposed conditions. In the matter of moving components, or groups of components, to achieve a "better" layout, the computer is usually only able to try all moves exhaustively, and this may be a lengthy and costly process even with a powerful machine. A good and practised designer can often spot a good move quickly; certainly he can use his judgement as to whether any change, or number of changes, has been sufficiently advantageous for him to call a halt and finalize the design.

Figure 1.3 shows detail of a finished design, printed out for checking on an electrostatic printer/plotter. When this has been approved, a further automatic process produces paper tapes for input to an automatic artwork table.

REDAL 30:System Design Aids. More recently REDAC Software Ltd. have produced some additional even more sophisticated graphics programs which add to the possibilities of the PCB design program. Provisionally entitled REDAL 30, the first program permits a designer to enter a rough sketch diagram, which may be in geometric or logic form. This can then be amplified and edited interactively. In logic form a sketch can be handled with up to 110 logic gates symbols, with associated connections, numbered terminals, and text. The next part of the program generates a parts list and stores the sketch for further use.

Stemming from REDAL 30 are two "post-processor" programs. The first of these allows the completed and checked logic or circuit diagram to be

Fig. 1.3 Electrostatically plotted final design from the REDAL 3/14 program.

entered into REDAL 3/14, the PCB layout program described above. The second prepares the data for drawing and instigates the production of a detailed engineering drawing or circuit diagram.

It is interesting to note that the drawing can be made to a precision of 1 in 32,000; that is, on a graticule of 32,000 by 32,000 spots. This illustrates one feature of interactive graphics; this precision is many times greater than the best precision to which the human can operate visually through the medium of the display unit (except by using the WINDOW facility). It should also be noticed how, in the design of the whole REDAL system, only those parts of the program which need interaction form the graphics system. A great deal more purely automatic activity is processed without reference to the interactive graphics terminal.

Architectural Graphics

An effective interactive graphics application has been developed by the West Sussex County Council, Chichester, England, for use in the County Architects' Department. This was brought into service in 1972; it supplanted an earlier experimental program developed in 1965 and embodies the lessons learned from prior experience (3).

In the first place, the site where building is proposed is inspected and surveyed in detail. The results are fed into the computer which files them for future use and can produce, on demand, a site map drawn by a digital plotter. Environmental details and any other relevant information may also be stored.

The architect commences work at the interactive console by indicating on a "menu" the type of project he is developing; for instance it might be a school. He can then start to sketch his preliminary design. When he has indicated the general shape of the building, and the requirements that he has in mind, he can check his scheme using the computer program. He can monitor the approximate cost, features such as heat loss and air change, and therefore running costs of the buildings, daylight factors, and the like. The advantage of graphics at this stage is that the designer can easily test alternative schemes and layouts so that he is reasonably sure of a good design.

Once the designer has determined this strategic design of the building, he proceeds to detailed development of the steelwork layout, external walls, partitions, and so on. Filed within the computer is a catalog of components and materials, with their specifications and limitations of use. Once the storey heights and type of building have been specified, then the computer restricts choice to those items which conform to the specification. At any stage a hard-copy plan can be drawn out on the plotter. Using a WINDOW technique the parts of the building under consideration can be scaled up or down. The designer can thus make detailed decisions about mechanical and electrical engineering, including items such as electric-light points and switches, heating devices, and other ironmongery. At any stage in the process the designer can call for a perspective, produced at the level of detail to which he has progressed. Figure 1.4 shows such a perspective image.

Items that can be shown include structural details and claddings, partitions, doors, and ceilings, together with fittings and sanitary, water, and electrical installations. The cataloged items are held in the computer with rules governing the computer's processing activities according to the circumstances of their use. For instance, the placing of a roof light on the CRT image will cause alterations to the whole computer-held model; it will deduct the area of the roof and finish required, generate the roof light in the ceiling plan of the room below, and also deduct from the ceiling area.

In support of the interactive display programs, as in the REDAL series, there is a range of automatic activity programs, for instance, for plotting and scaling the finished drawings, numbering them, and positioning them relative to each other and indicating overlaps. In addition the computer can print the necessary listings and work out the various costs, using rates and prices from lists which are continually updated.

This system is implemented on an IBM 360/155 with a 2250 graphics unit.

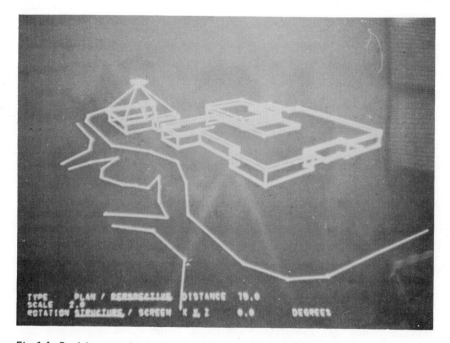

Fig. 1.4 Partial perspective image produced in an architectural application.

The ARK 2 System for Architectural Design

In constrast to the specialized program for use by county architects, Decision Graphics Inc. have produced a suite of architectural programs, entitled ARK 2, for more general use (4). This suite consists of eight programs, the first of which is broadly similar to the system described above, providing a model of a complete building, built up in detail and edited on the visual display. It can produce much the same kind of details of lists, inventories, and costs.

The next two programs are rather different, the first being in the form of a "bubble diagram" on which are entered relationships and functions of, for instance, the users of a projected building. The second program replaces the individual "bubbles" with suitable areas to accommodate the requirements called for by the functions, juxtaposing them in accordance with their interrelationships, but allowing the designer full powers to move, rotate, and adjust the individual blocks within the overall plan. At the same time it notes for later reference any changes made. This technique provides a powerful tool for laying out complicated, large-scale projects.

Two more programs of the suite are similar to the previous example, one giving display of three-dimensional views and perspectives and the other controlling the updating, merging, and scaling of drawings for output on a plotter or printer.

The remaining programs of the suite are of more general application, dealing with manipulation of sets of management goals, critical path analysis, and the handling and editing of manuals and other textual information.

ARK 2 is normally implemented on a DEC PDP 15/76 graphics system.

Both of these architectural systems illustrate the careful choice of what is to be dealt with by interactive graphics and what, within the overall system model held by the computer, need not be. The truly interactive graphics is a small proportion of the whole. A great deal of data-processing activity is carried out automatically by the main computing facilities, both to present the interactive image, and as a result of the decisions made using it. The more that can be specified within the model, restricting the number of possible alternatives, the more effective and fast the system can become for a specific purpose. On the other hand, the program ARK 2 illustrates that "architecture" does not only mean bricks and mortar. Typically, the program starting from the "bubble diagram" need not necessarily be applied to buildings, but could be used to aid the building of other structures; for instance, electronic components or microcircuits could be specified as the bubbles. The definition of their interrelationship would then lead to a placement routine as used in the design of PCB's. Once more it comes down to the fact that the images are still only dots, lines, characters, and simple shapes displayed in a particular topology for the human's consideration and decision.

Other Applications

It is not surprising that architects have been at the forefront in the development of computer graphics, as their work contains so much of the two elements of drawing and inventory which seem to fit so elegantly into the technique of computer graphics and data processing. A considerable number of programs have been written for computer graphics in architectural applications. As so often occurs in the field of computer programming, many of them have been less concerned with the overall problem than with particularly challenging aspects of it, such as perspective drawing and the automatic suppression of "hidden lines" (5).

It is natural, too, that circuit and logic designers have made efforts to exploit the technique. Enterprises that build computers and design graphics systems have had the facilities for graphics program development and have been able to see the possible advantages; they have been anxious to prove the value of their products. The problems they understand best have naturally been the first to undergo treatment. Thus, most computer manufacturers have developed sophisticated systems for their own use in circuit design, PCB layout, and component placement.

It is surprising, however, that there has been rather less effort to exploit the techniques of computer graphics in other fields. The aviation industry has been one exception to this; much work has been done by the major aircraft manufacturers using graphics as a design tool. These enterprises have been stimulated by ferocious competition. They have also been in a position to carry out expensive experiments to improve the cost effectiveness of their highly skilled design teams. Some aircraft manufacturers have evolved sophisticated techniques for in-house use and they have produced spectacular results. The design of aircraft is, in many ways, another form of architecture, so perhaps, in its present state of development, interactive graphics lends itself well to this field.

There are a number of areas where interesting experiments have been performed but techniques have not yet evolved enough for general acceptance. One such area is typography. A number of newspaper producers now use computer-editing techniques, and considerable work has been done to explore the use of graphics as an editing method and for "layout". In this area a limiting factor has been the low optical precision of the CRT display device. Another interesting area, explored by the author at Reading University, is that of typesetting sheet music by computer. The conventional musical notation is highly concentrated, from the information-theoretic point of view, and typesetting has, in the past, had to depend on the traditional arts of printing, engraving, and, especially, on human judgement. It was found at Reading University that typesetting of simple music could be conveniently dealt with

Fig. 1.5 Sample of digitally plotted music set by computer.

by a computer, provided that a good-quality graphics display was embodied in the system to allow intervention where human discretion was called for. Figure 1.5 shows a sample of music printed out by a digital plotter. It is noteworthy that this sample required several minutes drawing time on a high-speed incremental plotter. The quality of the printout is, however, amply satisfactory for photographic reproduction. It would take a very good quality CRT system to give a display of this precision.

Interactive graphics has been exploited in other areas where the human's drawing and estimating capabilities can be usefully employed. A notable example is in the development of magnet pole pieces for creating precisely defined magnetic fields, such as are required for plasma containment in nuclear-fusion experiments. Here the calculating power of the computer can be used in conjunction with the human skill at "relaxation methods" and similar drawing techniques.

A number of attempts have been made to reduce the human effort in cartoon animation by using computer graphics. Some of these have shown promise but little has yet been achieved.

An area which must surely develop as interactive graphics becomes cheaper and more sophisticated is that of engineering drawing, which is, after all, not far removed from architectural draughtsmanship. Programs now exist for converting the equivalent of engineers' sketches into complete drawings, and these will doubtless be improved and expanded. The interactive part of the technique is mostly connected with sketching. The computer generates the finished drawing on a precision graph plotter or drafting machine. When these systems have been fully developed they will be of immense value. Drawings can be stored on magnetic tape, and modifications and updates made without the labor of redrafting the whole diagram. Likewise, as in the architectural applications, the relationship between drawings and parts lists can be maintained by the computer, hopefully eliminating a common source of errors in this field!

It is easy to see the enormous potential of interactive graphics in industry and education. Before it makes its full impact, however, much must be done to improve its techniques and to make it cheap enough for many people to be able to afford to experiment with it. It is no more than a powerful tool; in order to reach its full potential it requires the genius of human users, who can see it as an aid to the solution of their problems and who have the skill and patience to develop it.

1.3. THE REQUIREMENTS OF AN INTERACTIVE COMPUTER GRAPHICS SYSTEM

Discussion of Applications

The systems which have been described form an illustrative cross section of interactive computer graphics in the present state of the art. It is quite appropriate to use the word "art" for, even more than the computer itself, computer graphics is a new technique and there is so much yet to be discovered about its possibilities and limitations.

From the simplest through to the most sophisticated application, it is apparent that what can be fairly called the computer graphics is a small part of the whole system. It is an input and output medium just as is the teletype. It is more powerful, certainly, but fundamentally it must belong to the same category. Just like the teletype, it requires a hardware interface to the computer, and it must be operated by a set of software subroutines used by applications programs. These subroutines are dedicated to it, and, if the system is to be general purpose, they must be independent of the task or application for which the system is to be used.

All current computer graphics systems are based on little more than was demonstrated on SKETCHPAD; the output images consist of dots and lines forming more or less simple shapes. The input of graphical data depends on the indication of positions in the field of operation, i.e., the display screen, whatever it may represent in a particular application.

The art of design of interactive computer-graphics systems is firstly to determine, for any application, which are the parts which are best treated by interaction with the computer, and secondly to translate these parts into a suitable form for communication with the computer. For instance, in the design of a printed-circuit board the required images are scale line drawings of the boards to be built. In the design of a servo system the Nyquist plot is chosen as a useful image. In the design of a bandpass filter the image chosen could be a circuit diagram or a frequency-response plot. Some engineers might prefer, in both these latter cases, to use a pole-zero plot. They are all graphs or simple line drawings made up of rows of dots; from the point of view of the designer, who is purely concerned with the "graphics", the choice is immaterial. The task of the designer of a general-purpose graphics system is to provide an efficient self-contained tool of hardware and software that will provide a communication medium for the object-program designer and the applications-problem solver.

Special-purpose systems will also always be needed, such as the radar-simulation devices used for training air traffic control personnel. The basic requirement remains, however, dots and lines, and the ability to manipulate them singly or in groups.

The Characteristics of a Visual Channel

It was stressed earlier that the telegram is for many purposes an inadequate means of communication. The reason for this is that it is slow. Although telegraph pulses are transmitted down wires at something approaching the speed of light, the amount of information that can be transmitted is small when compared with vocal or visual means of communication. Most of us realize this intuitively, but to appreciate and assess graphical communication it is necessary to delve more deeply and quantitatively into the study of information and its transmission[1].

The basic unit of information is called the *bit*, a contraction of the expression "binary unit". One definition of the bit is that it is the amount of information obtained when one of two possible *equally likely* alternative events occurs. In the context of computers we use the word "bit" as a contraction of the expression "binary digit". The digital information is held by two-state devices (bistables), each representing a *digital* bit. A digital bit can correspond to an information bit if its states are equiprobable, but in general this is not the case. A more accurate definition of the digital bit is that it is the smallest unit by which uncertainty about an event can be reduced. If we accept that our arguments will be approximate, then we can consider the two bits as equivalent. On this basis we shall be able to deduce enlightening comparisons between information transmission methods.

The presence or absence of a pulse at a predetermined time can specify one of two alternatives, for instance, the first or second half of an alphabet. A second pulse time, or epoch, can specify the first or second half of the previously specified half, and so on. Thus for an alphabet of 32 symbols, only five pulse epochs would be needed, since $2^5 = 32$. An additional pulse would allow 64 partitions of the alphabet, or, more generally, "universe of discourse". If any such universe can be divided into n partitions then $\log_2 n$ bits contain enough information to decide uniquely which partition is intended, in other words, to diminish the uncertainty completely. In an interactive computer-graphics system, there is a large discrepancy between the speeds of data flow in the two directions between man and machine. This is an important point.

[1] There is an established scientific discipline known as *information theory* which deals rigorously with information and its transmission. It repays the effort of serious study handsomely. Although its advanced concepts are sometimes difficult to grasp, its basic concepts are elegantly simple and provide useful insight into the practical problems of communication (6).

A commonly used interactive console is the teletype, which transmits data in groups of eight pulses, or pulse epochs. Thus each depression of a key imparts enough information to specify uniquely at the receiving end one of 256 characters. All possible combinations of the eight bits are not in fact used, and the universe of discourse or, in this case, the *character set,* is considerably smaller. The teletype transmission rate is about 10 characters per second; thus its theoretical maximum information rate would be 80 bit/s. For a variety of reasons the true information measure of the rate would be considerably less. For our purposes the rate of 80 bits or pulse periods per second will suffice.

Let us consider a speech channel. This analog transmission is described in terms of sinusoidal wave cycles per second, or Hertz, rather than pulses per second or *bauds* (the traditional telegraphy units). The human ear can detect signals with frequency components up to about 20 kHz (20,000 cycles per second). Marginally intelligible speech can be transmitted using frequency components up to about 500 Hz, but for a reasonably pleasant-sounding voice and acceptable intelligibility, telephone channels usually employ a *bandwidth* greater than 2 kHz. The bandwidth of a channel gives an indication of the highest frequency component transmitted. In order to compare the rate of transfer of information or speech with the teletype we must convert the sounds into pulses. This is often done for long-distance transmission of speech using a technique known as *pulse-code modulation* (PCM). Acceptable results are obtained if analog samples are taken about 10,000 times per second and converted into 6 or 7 digital bits. This means that the total transfer rate of a digital speech-transmission system must be 60,000 or 70,000 bits/s. High-fidelity musical reproduction requires a transmission rate 10 times as high again. It should be noted, however, that these are digital bit rates; the information content of a spoken message is nothing like as high as this. A good comparison of information transfer rates is the difference in speed between the teletype printing out a message and a human speaking the same words. Experienced teletype users will realize that the voice is at least twice as fast.

Let us now consider a visual channel, say the "video" channel of television. The standard "frame" consists of 525 lines in the USA and 625 lines in Europe. Since the image is oblong, we can obtain approximately the same definition in the horizontal and vertical directions if we describe each line as the equivalent of 1000 dots. Let us suppose there are eight permitted colors or intensities for a point; then a 3-bit code would be required to specify each dot. For one frame we would have to transmit

$$525 \times 1000 \times 3 \text{ bits} = 1,575,000 \text{ bits (in the USA)}$$

or

$$625 \times 1000 \times 3 \text{ bits} = 1,875,000 \text{ bits (in Europe)}.$$

This would have to be transmitted 25 or 30 times per second according to whether the European or American standard frame rates were used. Both of these require about 47 million bits/s. This is a huge figure, but we should note four things. Firstly, the actual information content of a television transmission is far less than the figure quoted. Secondly, present television broadcasting techniques do not depend on digital transmission and the transmitted information is ingeniously compressed into a bandwidth of about 5 MHz. Thirdly, however we calculate it or transmit it, the visual-channel capability for information transfer is hundreds of times greater than that of a speech channel and thousands of times greater than that of a telegraph channel. Fourthly, if we envisage a completely computer-generated television image, in color or graded shades between black and white, we must also envisage a computer of considerably more power than is available today.

The figures derived above are approximate, but they do convey the relative importance of parts of the communication problem. Interactive graphics is not only a matter of machines but also of people. The rates at which humans can absorb and process visual and aural data are a matter of study for perception psychologists. They pose formidable problems of measurement or even estimation. For all that, the interactive graphics system designer must bear them in mind and make intelligent assessments of them. In the end, a graphics system will be judged by a user who will either like it or not. His judgement may well be more subjective than objective.

Man–Machine Communication

The important point that comes from the foregoing estimations of data rates is that a visual image that a human can see, and which a computer must generate, may carry information at a much greater rate than we are able to transmit into the computer. If interactive graphics is to be efficient, our strategy for man–machine communication must be based on this. In order to suit the human, our interaction will need to be in "real time"; that is, when the human has decided what to do, what questions to ask, or what he wants the computer to do, the computer must respond promptly. The user wants the image he is watching to give the information called for while the subject is still foremost in his mind. This requires organization.

A simple example will illustrate this strategy. Let us suppose that the task in which the man and machine are to interact is some kind of information search or editing process. In the first place, if the information on which the work is to be done is of any great volume, it will take a long time to transmit it into the computer. At some stage it will have to be typed via a keyboard onto tape, cards, or some similar medium. It can then be transmitted to the computer and stored. It is only after this has been done that useful interaction can take place. Because of the computer's speed in data manipulation, and the speed of the cathode-ray oscilloscope, the computer can call data from store and display it as text very quickly. The human need only type in a short coded message, say a page number, and the computer can immediately display the text of the page called for. The indication of the page number may be adequate as an input message, or there may be a key which, when pressed, causes the computer to display the next page. A carefully organized code will allow short keyboard messages to be interpreted by the computer, in the context of the applications program, as commands to perform the editing or sorting functions that the human requires. It is useful to keep in mind the logical concept of the universe of discourse. The more alternative actions the computer "knows" about, the more ambiguity it needs to have resolved and the more information it needs for this resolution. A few binary bits can resolve a great deal of ambiguity, if the data within the computer is suitably stored. When the input and output data rates are appreciated, the strategy becomes obvious. Firstly, let the computer ask the questions and indicate a choice of possible answers. Then let the human indicate which answer is appropriate. Only when the computer has not been programmed to hold an appropriate answer does the human need to input a large quantity of information, with the inevitable penalty of delay and slower operation.

There is another important aspect of interactive graphics that must be borne in mind, that of human behavior and capability. A human, performing detailed work and interacting with a computer, will require watching and thinking time as a result of each new computer-generated picture. This is sometimes aptly called head-scratching time. These times may seem short in human terms but they are long for the computer. This is one reason why interactive graphics for many purposes is only economic if the system is time shared. A computer is able to service many terminals if the humans working on them take time to think. The work of a few microseconds by the computer can give the human cause for seconds, or even minutes, of thought. Even in "geometrical" interaction, when the human is drawing images into the computer, this ratio still applies although, depending on the nature of the drawing, perhaps to a lesser extent. Because time affects system operation, an experiment to analyze the human response time in interactive graphical operations was carried out at the European Centre for Nuclear Research (7). Briefly, the results showed that 50% of the responses occur in less than 4.5 s, while 90% occur in less than 16 s. Examination of the published graphs shows that few response times were less than 1.5 s. It is sensible to take two or three seconds as a "normal" human response time for design considerations.

One final point must be mentioned concerning the nature of graphical communication. The human visual channel is such an adept processor of information that it has always been used for the appreciation of complex data. Diagrams, maps, and writing are traditional graphical devices invented to exploit visual processing power. However, the situation is entirely one way, *into* the human visual channel. We are not so good at graphical output, and in fact we have to monitor our output efforts by reinputting them continuously so as to see what we are doing. It is difficult to draw a circuit diagram without looking at it; if we cannot look at it we visualize it. It is almost impossible to draw without looking or visualizing. This point is important when dealing with graphical input, and shows the necessity for immediately repeating the input on the output channel. Only light pens do not need this, since their position on the display can be directly seen, although later discussion of these devices will show the need for a repeated cursor in tracking applications.

REFERENCES

1. Sutherland, I. E. SKETCHPAD: a man–machine graphical communication system. *Proc. SJCC 1963,* p. 329. Spartan Books, Baltimore, Md.
2. Atkinson, P. Computer-aided design of closed loop control systems. *Comp. Aided Design,* **4**, 120–128, April 1972.
3. Patterson, J. An integrated c.a.d. system for an architect's department. *Comp. Aided Design,* **6**(1), 25–32, Jan. 1974.
4. Digital Equipment Corporation, Maynard, Mass. *Profit Making Graphics,* 1973.
5. Greenburg, D. P. Computer graphics in architecture. *Sci. Amer.* **230**(5), 98, May 1974.
6. Shannon, C. E., and Weaver, W. *A Mathematical Theory of Communication.* University of Illinois Press, Urbana, Ill., 1949.
7. Yule, A. Human response times in a graphic environment. *Brit. Comp. Soc. Comp. Bull.* **16**(6), 304–305, June 1972.

Basic Elements of Interactive Computer Graphics Systems

2.1. INTRODUCTION

Whether interactive or not, the first and most obvious requirement of a computer graphics system is a display. In all the examples we have considered the display element is a *cathode-ray tube,* or *CRT.* For reasons that will be discussed later, the CRT in one form or another is the universal graphic display device.

In order to position a spot on a CRT, horizontal and vertical (x and y) deflection voltages must be supplied to it in analog form, in proportion to the deflections required. Likewise the brightness must be controlled by an externally supplied voltage ("Z modulation"). In simple systems only two levels of brightness are needed, bright-up, or zero. More sophisticated systems have a range of a few discrete values; some have a continuous range from zero to maximum. Data within the computer is in the form of binary number patterns; hence there must be *digital-to-analog* (*D–A*) conversion of the appropriate precision and speed to supply the *x, y,* and *z* voltages for the CRT.

The most versatile CRTs are simple ones which produce only fleeting images. In order to give the impression of a continuous picture. the image must be retraced repeatedly many times per second. This may be done, as in the original SKETCHPAD, by recalculating and redrawing the image. A computer is fast enough to do this, but it is wasting time and reducing its availability for more useful activity. Modern systems are arranged to take most of the task of image refresh off the mainframe computer either by using a small fast dedicated front-end machine or by the provision of special hardware for display control. The simple system described earlier for Nyquist-plot generation maintains the image as well as calculating the points on the graph. It can do this only because the displayed image is a simple one (two lines and about 100 points). For a more complex task the small computer could perhaps maintain the image or do the calculations but not both.

The sequence of computer instructions for displaying a spot on the CRT screen is a simple one: (i) generate x and y coordinates; (ii) convert them to voltages; (iii) generate bright-up; (iv) repeat many times per second (the frequency of repetition depends on factors which will be discussed later). To generate a straight line or *vector*, the process is modified to give x and y increments, thereby generating successive spots along the line; this whole process, performed repeatedly, gives a continuous image. Characters may be generated as sets of dots by simple subroutines, but it is common to use special hardware *character generators* to speed up the process. Generation of a whole image is merely concatenation of the simple processes of dot, line, and character generation in a suitable order. It will be apparent that the result is no longer simple.

A complicated image will call for a long list of coordinate data and character descriptions. Owing to the physical characteristics of the CRT and D-A converters there are also timing requirements to be considered. Because of the complexity of the process it is necessary to have an operating system, either in software or in microprogrammed form, to deal with the display and maintain it. Nowadays this is implemented in hardware and called the *display processor.* (There are some simple devices which display a contiguous set of store locations in fixed format. These are known as *display channels.*)

Customarily the data to describe the image to be displayed is maintained in computer store as the *display file.* When the computer is running the program for the relevant application (i.e., the *user program* or *applications program*), it makes alterations or additions to the contents of the display file. The display processor reads data from the display file and executes the operations required to display the corresponding picture; it also refreshes images as often as required. The display file is a flexible structure of data which can be continuously changed by the user program specifying the image; the display processor is a set of actions which may be program controlled.

If the graphics is to be interactive there must also be an input channel so that the user can communicate to the computer. From the applications described in the previous chapter it is apparent that this channel is much simpler than the output channel. Broadly, all that is required of the input channel is some device that allows the user of the system to indicate points or areas on the display. It needs to be little more than this; for instance, in the REDAC application, if the user points to the menu instruction MOVE he is merely indicating to the computer the area in which MOVE is written. The applications program relates this position to the process called for by the MOVE instruction. It is necessary to call the attention of the system to the fact that the user is pointing and to give certain option-selection instructions. For these, switches and push buttons are used to control *flags,* or status indications, which the user program scans and interprets. Keyboards may also be necessary to transmit numerical or textual information about a picture.

In any interactive graphics system the main applications program may well be voluminous. The program and associated data are entered into the system by conventional high-speed storage devices (magnetic- or paper-tape readers). The only information that is taken into the system through the graphics channel should be that needed for the activities of interaction. For an efficient system this information should be of the simplest form.

We can enumerate the essentials of an interactive graphics system by their function, as follows.

Output: Display
          Coordinate conversion
          Display maintenance or "refresh"
          Display processor
          Display file
Input: Position indication (or pointing device)
          Control and "call" switches
          Keyboard

The graphics only furnishes an input–output medium. There must be an information interface between this and the applications program, just as there must be a hardware interface between the display unit and the main computer. The information interface is vested in the display file. The hardware interface will depend on many things, not the least of which will be cost. These interfaces and the system elements form the subject matter of the remainder of this text.

2.2. THE CATHODE-RAY TUBE AS A DISPLAY ELEMENT

Introduction

The CRT is physically large and requires high-voltage supplies; in a world of miniaturization and microelectronics it would be surprising if there were not efforts to develop a substitute for it, but up to now it has had no real competitors. There are some interesting pattern displays which show promise, but they are, as yet, a long way from being satisfactory output devices for a general-purpose graphics system. They have mostly been developed alongside the alphanumeric devices so much in demand for electronic calculators. Naturally the manufacturers and designers of CRT's are aware of these developments; they are continually investigating a number of avenues of possible improvement, especially storage tubes and cathodochromic displays. It seems likely that the CRT, in one form or another, will continue to be the universal output-display device for computer graphics for some years yet. It will require a technological advance of "breakthrough" status to displace it.

The nature and principles of operation of CRT's are well described in texts on electronics. There are some features of CRT's, however, which impose important constraints on the design of computer graphics systems.

In the first place, the basic CRT produces a fleeting image; this implies that, in order to maintain a steady picture, the pattern on the screen must be continually refreshed. In different applications this may be done under software control, or by a hardware system, or by the special design of the tube itself. Each method has its own characteristics, merits, and demerits, and a reasoned choice must be made from them to suit the applications for which a particular system is to be designed.

The Optical System

The human optical system depends on the generation of chemical substances in the cells of the retina at the back of the eye when light falls on them. These chemical processes have characteristic time constants which are long in comparison with those of computer electronics. These time constants make for the phenomenon of *persistence* of vision.

Cinema and television show that a brightly illuminated image appears continuous if it is repeated about 25 or 30 times per second. Memories of the old cinema convince us that similar images repeated 16 times per second give a flickering effect that is just tolerable. Generally, the brighter the image the less frequently it needs to be refreshed. We need no special field trials or laboratory experiments to establish that, for reasonably bright images and normal eyesight, an image refreshed in excess of 20 times per second is acceptable to watch. We must remember that in computer graphics applications some people may have to spend long periods closely watching the display. When it comes to the consideration of "refresh rate" it is good policy to err on the high side.

It is also known that in viewing bright light the parts of the retina which are affected by it can be drained of the chemical known as "visual purple"; the image remains on the retina for a painfully long time causing temporarily blind areas and disagreeable color effects. In the consideration of display brightness, it is better to err on the low side.

The manufacturers of CRT's have given considerable attention to the problems of brightness and flicker; their approach to its solution is by the careful choice of *phosphors,* that is, the substances that are coated on the inside of the tube face to transform the electron-beam energy into visible light.

Phosphors

The technology of phosphors for CRT's is very specialized. Different materials give a wide range of intensity and persistence over a spectrum of colors. They are catalogued under a range of about 40 P numbers according to their color and persistence; the numbers are merely identifying labels and have no other significance. Phosphor P1, for instance, is a yellowish-green medium-persistence phosphor of no particular importance. Phosphor P4, on the other hand, is white, with a persistence of about 60 μs and is very important for television. Phosphor P16 is bluish-purple and has an extremely short persistence of about .1 us; P34 is bluish-green with a very long persistence of 100 s. This latter pair give an idea of the persistence range. Phosphors have other characteristics that need to be watched in system design; some can give a constant bright spot without suffering, whereas others, typically the long-persistence ones, can be easily damaged by over-bombardment if a high-energy beam is allowed to dwell in one place for long.

An important consideration in the choice of phosphor for computer graphics is that the spectral response of the eye is not uniform. The eye is much more sensitive to light in the yellow region of the spectrum. Photocells and other photosensitive devices also have widely varying spectral sensitivities and speeds. Thus the intended use of a light pen further complicates the problem, as will be discussed later.

Usually the phosphors deposited on tube faces are a mixture of different materials with complementary characteristics. Some CRT's have, as a basic phosphor, one that gives a high intensity of light output quickly, such as P16, which if used on its own does not give a very attractive color. The high-intensity light output acts on other phosphors in the mixture which are less sensitive to electron bombardment but give out more suitably colored light when bombarded by photons from the first phosphor. Most basic phosphor materials have exponential characteristics both for illumination and decay. Efforts are made to combine phosphors to give a plateau form of decay characteristic in order to try and arrange for the light output to remain substantially constant for a short time after bombardment (the "drop-dead" type of characteristic as it is sometimes called).

The long-persistence phosphors give out mostly red or orange light; these are used for applications such as radar displays where the interval between refreshes is necessarily slow. These phosphors, in subdued light, give a clear image over the whole period of rotation of a large antenna. It might seem that these long-persistence phosphors could supply a partial answer to the flicker problem, but this is not so. Interactive graphics calls for images to be erased, modified, and moved quickly. A phosphor having too long a persistence causes ghost images to remain after such activities.

The use of a light pen leads to problems apart from color sensitivity. The light pen depends for its operation on detecting the presence of the light-emitting spot on the tube face. If this spot does not appear often enough, or if it is not bright enough, then the light-pen technique will not work. Flicker is reduced by causing the spot to have a long "afterglow". For an agreeable image (for human viewing), the initial brightness should not be high or else it blinds the viewer. On the other hand, the light pen must not detect the afterglow. Hence a compromise solution needs to be found. The human viewer can be aided by the interposition of a suitable colored filter screen over the face of the tube to reduce the intensity of the initial spot compared with the afterglow; this militates against a light pen's requirements.

In order to use the illumination from the phosphor to the best advantage most tubes today have an aluminum film deposited on the back of the phosphor. This intensifies the light output from the tube as well as providing an easy discharge path for charges built up by the electron beam, giving the system more speed and consistent behavior.

Today there are a number of graphics displays using color techniques. One obvious way of achieving this is to use a *television* or television *monitor* tube since these have been highly developed, and are good value for money because they are mass produced. Monitors are quite easy to adapt if, as is commonly the case, the color-gun drives are brought out.

A color system of use for graphics has been developed to work on a different principle from the conventional television (TV) shadow-mask or trinitron types of tube. This tube, the "penetron" (Westinghouse Corporation: Penetration Control tube for Multicolor Display, WX-32337PX73), depends on the deposition of the different color phosphors in successive layers on the tube face. The phosphor, and hence color, that is energized by the electron beam depends on the depth of penetration by the bombarding electrons. This depth is a direct function of the accelerating potential. Color variation is thus dependent on the control of the EHT[1] voltage; this is not a trivial control problem, though, fortunately, not one for the graphics system or designer.

CRT Deflection Systems

The conventional general-purpose CRT for laboratory use is almost invariably controlled by an electrostatic deflection system. The display area is usually small and the resolution of the image is low. The resolution of a display system is closely analogous to the precision of a measuring system. Broadly it indicates a comparison between the size of the best focused dot and the largest image that can be displayed. For laboratory work, such as monitoring electronic waveforms, a resolution of about 1% is adequate. Higher-grade instruments are available for measurement and similar activities, but these are costly and somewhat specialized.

Large displays such as those used for TV and radar are nearly always electromagnetically deflected. These give a much better resolution and picture definition than their laboratory counterparts. A domestic TV display registers 500 or 600 distinguishable lines vertically and its horizontal resolution may be estimated at about the same. There are precision displays and monitors that have a resolution several times better than this.

The principles of electrostatic and electromagnetic deflection systems are amply described elsewhere (1, 2). Certain of their characteristics, however, impose constraints on the design of graphic display systems.

An important point is image size; generally computer graphics displays are required to be fairly large so that the user or operator can view them at a comfortable distance and, often, so that several people can view them simultaneously.

It is shown in texts on CRT's that the deflection sensitivity of electrostatic systems is inversely proportional to the accelerating potential; in electromagnetic systems it is inversely proportional to the square root of the accelerating potential. It is difficult to use electrostatic deflection systems for large display tubes since EHT voltages of as much as 20 kV would be needed to obtain the largest deflections. Laboratory CRT's use "post-deflection acceleration" to solve this problem, but this leads to poor focusing and reduced resolution. Thus electromagnetic tubes are generally chosen for graphical displays since they give good resolution over a large image. They are also cheaper than electrostatic tubes.

The cheapness of the electromagnetic tube stems from the fact that it has a much simpler electrode structure. In the manufacture of electrostatic tubes

---

[1] The extra-high-tension (or EHT) voltage provides the accelerating potential for the electron beam.

the electron lens, focusing electrodes, and deflection electrodes are set up within the tube envelope prior to vacuum pumping. The electromagnetic tube has only its electron gun within the evacuated-tube envelope. The focusing and deflection is achieved by coils placed around the neck of the tube. These can be removed, changed, or adjusted while the tube is operating. Likewise, if the tube is replaced, they can remain *in situ*. Furthermore, since the conventional TV tube is of this construction, electromagnetic tubes for display purposes can benefit from the advantages of large-quantity production.

In order to generate the high field strengths required for electromagnetic deflection, the coils must have appreciable inductance; a typical TV scan coil may have an inductance of 25 mH. This imposes a time constant on the deflection system, thus limiting the speed of the display. A reasonably good quality graphics display has a maximum "slew rate" of about 1 cm/μs and this imposes timing conditions on the display program. In many systems the display is generated by setting the x and y coordinate values into the display as voltage step functions. If a coordinate step makes the beam traverse a large part of the screen, the display will require a settling time of perhaps 20 or 30 μs before bright-up can be permitted. Customarily the way this problem is solved is for the display unit to put out a status "busy" indication while the current in the deflection coils is being established. In this way the display program can detect when it is time to give the bright-up signal.

2.3. TECHNIQUES OF CONSTANT IMAGE MAINTENANCE

Storage Tubes

The *direct view storage tube* (*DVST*) is one ingenious solution of the problem of the CRT's fleeting image. It was not originally developed as a solution to the flicker problem but to study "one-shot" waveforms, such as transient discharges and contact bounce, which are not repetitive.

Basically the DVST is constructed like a conventional electrostatically controlled CRT but with an additional grid electrode and a second electron gun. The additional electron gun provides a broad low-energy beam of electrons and is called a *flood gun*. The grid electrode is normally formed of fine wires spaced as closely as 250 per inch and is placed near the tube viewing face. The surface of this grid remote from the viewing face is coated with a film of good insulator. Some manufacturers, notably Tektronix, have managed to deposit what corresponds to this grid electrode as an integral part of the phosphor deposition, giving a *bistable phosphor*.

The principle of operation of the storage tube depends on the phenomena of *secondary emission* due to electron bombardment. Suitable materials have a secondary-emission coefficient that is less than unity for beam energies below a few hundred volts, rising to two or three over a range of some thousands of volts, and then falling below unity again as the "second crossover voltage" is exceeded. The insulated grid has a high secondary-emission constant. When it is bombarded by the tightly focused high-energy beam from the "write" electron gun it loses more electrons than it gains, becoming positively charged in areas where the beam strikes it. Hence a positive-charge pattern is generated corresponding to the track of the writing beam.

Immediately prior to writing, a sequence of voltages is applied to the grid mesh leaving it negatively charged with respect to the gun cathodes. In this state the low-energy, or flood, beam is prevented from impinging on the tube face. When the writing beam sets up the positive-charge pattern on the grid surface, the positively charged areas accelerate the flood-gun electrons through the grid mesh and these cause illumination of the viewing surface in correspondence to the stored charge pattern on the grid electrode. The electrons which are repelled from the grid are collected on a collector electrode or on the tube walls. The flood-gun electrons have little effect on the charge pattern on the storage grid so that the image can be retained for many minutes without deterioration.

Manipulation of the grid and drive voltages allows setting up for writing and for total image erasure by flooding. The principal disadvantages of the storage tube are (i) that it cannot be selectively erased, that is, parts of the image cannot be individually deleted, and (ii) that a light pen will not work since continuous refresh is not used. The fine-grain tubes which do not use a wire grid allow a high-definition image to be written and are particularly useful in applications like text editing, where thousands of legible characters have to be displayed. These tubes have a low light output which entails operating them in an environment of subdued lighting. By control of the write-gun voltage it is possible to write on the viewing screen in the normal repetitive refresh mode without storing the image; this allows a cursor figure to be used and data to be displayed temporarily until the operator is satisfied that it is correct.

The tubes fitted with the discrete grid electrode give better illumination and can be used satisfactorily in a brightly lit environment. They cannot have a resolution better than the mesh of the grid and, naturally, fine-mesh tubes are costly.

Cathodochromic Display Tubes

Some phosphors that can be deposited on CRT faces change color under electron bombardment; these are used in *cathodochromic displays*. The original color can be restored by light or heat according to the material used. Research is going on into this type of display as the deposition is easy and no complicated or expensive extra electrodes or grids are needed in manufacture. These displays have the added advantage that they can be used in "projection mode"; in this mode an intense external light source is focused on the tube face and the image is reflected from it onto a diffuse rear projection screen. This screen can be considerably larger than is practicable for a conventional CRT face plate, which is limited to about 25 in. Since the image is reflective, the cathodochromic display gives good contrast in high ambient light.

Like the direct-view storage tube, the major development problem is with erasure, particularly selective erasure. Erasure by light is accomplished by brief bursts of light generated by flash tubes focused on the screen; this complicates the display arrangement because this flash must not be transmitted to the viewer. Thermal erasure is also an inconvenient process; an electron beam can, however, heat the phosphor at the point of bombardment and this offers the possibility of selective erasure. Research is in progress to develop this technique (3). One of the difficulties encountered is that an erased spot becomes surrounded by a colored area.

If the erasure problems of the cathodochromic display tube can be solved, it could well become an ideal device for many kinds of computer graphics, including the interactive.

Image Generation and Regeneration by Continuous Repetition

Interactive graphics demands selective erasure. Since the storage tube still has severe limitations in this respect, there is no alternative to using a conventional CRT and redrawing the image continuously. Whatever the technique of repeated image generation, the problem is simplified if the image is made easier to draw; the topic of image generation, therefore, is inseparable from that of image regeneration or "refresh".

It was pointed out in Chapter 1 that even the most sophisticated system generates images that consist of dots, lines, and simple shapes, albeit a great number of them in some complicated applications. A principal stratagem for reducing the effort required in generating an image is to provide hardware devices to generate the standard patterns. Typical of these are vector and character generators. Other function generators are available for curves and circles. All these generators have been developed based on both analog and digital techniques.

The major drawback of having to redraw the image continuously is that it must be stored somewhere in its entirety and, if it is a complicated image, it may require a large amount of fast storage. If the image is drawn and redrawn in analog form, that is, from point to point on the screen defined by x and y coordinates, the stored data for the image must be available quickly, but at arbitrary times, depending on the nature of the image being drawn and on the necessity of synchronizing to the time delays in the deflection system.

If an image can be drawn in, or converted to, a raster type of display like that of TV, then regeneration can be performed serially at a fixed speed. This allows fast serial stores to be used, and these are generally cheaper than random-access stores and are also simpler to organize. It must be remembered that the amount of storage required for this kind of image is always the maximum; every dot on every line of the raster must be stored. Before long, large-scale-integration semiconductor techniques (*LSI*) will make long shift registers cheaply enough to be used as image regeneration stores for this kind of graphics. For the past few years rotating stores such as high-speed magnetic discs have been used economically to store high-resolution images. For low-resolution images such as alphanumeric displays on VDU's, the MSI store is now well established, having replaced the delay lines on which reliance had to be placed for several years.

2.4. DIGITAL-TO-ANALOG AND ANALOG-TO-DIGITAL CONVERSION

Introduction

There are many areas of computer graphics in which D-A or A-D conversion is needed. There are several techniques by which it can be accomplished and a considerable number of converters on the market.

Digital–analog and analog–digital converters are designed and manufactured for a variety of applications; graphics is not usually one of these because the requirements of converters for graphics are somewhat different from those of more common applications. This makes the choice of the "best" device quite difficult.

Normally the designers of converters have three main targets: speed, accuracy, and linearity. These are the qualities needed in their main applications such as measurement, on-line control, and communications. Devices are obtainable that are (i) fast enough for the operations of pulse coding of TV data, and (ii) accurate and linear enough for laboratory measurement and precision-machine control. The users of such devices are prepared to pay the high prices that this performance demands, and it is hardly surprising that enterprising manufacturers concentrate their efforts on this kind of device.

The requirements of converters for graphics are not stringent compared with the standards of these high-performance converters. In displays, D-A converters are required to generate the primary x and y coordinate deflections along with secondary deflections derived from character and function generators; commonly a converter is also needed for control of brightness.

Analog–digital conversion is required to convert analog position information from input devices into digital form suitable for transmission to the computer. Each of these uses makes different demands on the conversion device.

The X-Y display is to be watched by human eyes and needs only to be good enough to present a satisfactory image for viewing. The converter must be fast enough to drive the display device at its maximum speed. Because most display devices are electromagnetically deflected, the system speed limitation derives from the deflection time constants rather than from the conversion device. A D-A converter of quite modest speed capability is satisfactory.

The accuracy of a D-A converter is related to its precision or resolution. A high-quality graphics image may be displayed on a matrix of 4000 dots in each direction. Because of the human *vernier acuity*, adjacent dots are visually separable. Thus, the converter for x and y deflection requires a resolution of 1 in 4000; that is, 12 bits. This is equal to the best guaranteed resolution of all but the most specialized D-A converters. The 12-bit limitation arises from the theoretical noise value of the components of the converter compared with the size of the smallest measurable interval (4). On this basis the converter for graphics use needs to be of very high performance.

The accuracy of a D-A converter is also related to its linearity. Another characteristic of the human visual capability is its poor accuracy in judgement of linear dimensions of images in different parts of an image field. If the eye is intentionally deluded it can tolerate errors of 10% or more. Even a skilled eye is unlikely to detect a discrepancy of 1% in two lengths at different ends of an image field. Few people could detect the error in a circle with the vertical and horizontal diameters differing by 1%. Thus the overall linearity of a conversion device need be no better than 1%. Measurement converters frequently have linearity specifications 10 times as great. Even for sophisticated systems Z modulation is restricted normally to eight "grey levels"; hence conversion is required to a precision of 3 bits.

Input device A-D converters require the same kind of precision or resolution as the x and y deflection converters. If a cursor-spot technique is used as the operating mode, as is the case with resistive tablets and joystick inputs, the linearity called for is very low, since the human visual feedback loop adjusts for even severe non-linearities when moving the cursor across the screen.

These considerations show that it is possible to select devices suitable for use in graphical applications. Available devices which are good enough in one respect are usually better than they need be in others, and for this reason the choice is not always economical. Often it is better to build a converter specially for a graphics system; the type of converter should always be considered carefully.

Techniques of D-A Conversion

There is a wealth of detailed literature on D-A conversion devices (5). A brief examination of common techniques is useful in this text. A knowledge of such characteristics is always helpful in choosing the most suitable device for an application.

There are three commonly used techniques of digital-to-analog conversion. Analog-to-digital conversion is achieved by using digital-to-analog devices connected in a feedback configuration. The simplest D-A method, inconcept, is called the *weighted-resistor* method. Figure 2.1 shows a circuit which illustrates the principle of operation, capable of D-A conversion to 4 bits precision. The four binary inputs operate switches connected to the input terminal of an operational amplifier through resistors having values $8R$, $4R$, $2R$ and R. The operational amplifier of gain A is sign reversing, has a high input impedance, and is assumed to draw negligible input current. A feedback resistor is connected across the operational amplifier and has the value R.

If the amplifier gain A is high, for the output voltage to be finite, the input voltage must be negligibly small; that is, the point X in Fig. 2.1 is a virtual earth. If a voltage V is applied to the input terminal, the current into the circuit must be given by V/R, $V/2R$, $V/4R$, or $V/8R$. Since the amplifier draws no current, all current from the input must flow through the feedback resistor. The output voltage will be developed across this resistor and will be $V_0 = iR$ where i is the sum of the currents contributed by the inputs. The output voltage will be the sum of the input voltages divided by the resistance ratios, that is, $V/8$, $V/4$, $V/2$, and V. If these inputs are switched in by four binary digits of significance 1, 2, 4, and 8, then V_0 will be a voltage proportional to their binary value.

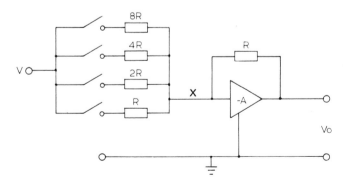

Figure 2.1. Weighted=resistor D-A converter.

Although this system is simple in concept it is difficult to make it work to high precision. Let us suppose the precision required is 12 bits; the largest weighted resistor will need to be 4096 times the magnitude of the smallest. If conversion is to be linear to the least significant bit, this resistor's permitted error, or *tolerance,* cannot exceed a value of one-half of the smallest resistor value. Thus the largest-valued resistor will have to be constructed to a precision of about 1 part in 10,000, which is difficult indeed. However, it is a trivial exercise to design a converter of this kind working to 3 bits precision for use as a Z-modulation control, or to work in a character generator as described later in this chapter.

The most commonly used technique for high-speed and high-precision converters is to use a *resistive ladder.* Figure 2.2 shows the arrangement of such a circuit. Elementary circuit theory shows that V_1 equals $V_2/2$. The resistance to the right of the node at which V_2 is measured is $2R$ in parallel with $2R$, that is, R. Thus V_2 must be half V_3 and, likewise, V_3 must be half V_4. This ladder can be extended indefinitely and the voltage at each node, going towards the input, will be twice that of the one before. If these voltages are switched into the input of a summing amplifier by binary digits of the appropriate significance, the summed output voltage will be the analog value of the digital input.

This system does not suffer from the same magnitude problem as the weighted-resistor method since only two values of resistor are required. Tolerance limitations are still severe but ladder-type converters are commonly available to 12 bits precision. They are also highly linear but costly owing to the stringent design requirements of the electronic switches and the summing amplifier.

A third technique of conversion is the ramp method. Once more the principle is simple. An integrating amplifier is supplied with pulses of regulated amplitude and duration. The output voltage thus formed is a linear ramp; the amplitude at any time is a linear function of the number of pulses received. If the pulses are supplied from a steady clock-pulse source and simultaneously counted, the output voltage at any

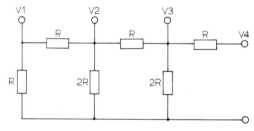

Figure 2.2. Resistive-ladder network.

instant is porportional to the count value. If the counter is binary and the ramp is stopped at a desired binary count, the output voltage will be its analog value. Likewise, if the count is stopped when the output voltage reaches a preset analog value, the counter will register the binary equivalent of this preset value, giving A-D conversion.

In order to obtain high accuracy and linearity a converter of this kind requires precise control of the ramp generator and the amplitude and duration of the input pulses. On the other hand, the number of pulses to give full-scale output (and hence the resolution) can be easily increased, merely causing the ramp increments to be smaller. If the linearity requirement is not stringent, this technique can be used to give high resolution either in D-A or A-D form. Bearing in mind the low linearity requirement of a graphics display it is not difficult to design an adequate D-A converter using a ramp, though at current prices it may well be advantageous to use a commercial device. With the less stringent linearity requirements of input devices, however, it is often simpler and cheaper to design the A-D conversion as a part of the system electronics. This is especially the case if the display is of the TV scan type, since both vertical and horizontal ramp voltages already exist within the display unit for controlling the scan. The use of these voltages to provide the ramps for A-D conversion allows a simple, efficient, and economical input device to be designed.

An extension of this technique is to use a *binary-rate multiplier*. This device, much used in hybrid computing, is available in MSI. Its characteristic is that it emits pulses at a frequency defined by the binary number set into its internal control register. Thus, if its output is applied to an integrating amplifier, it will generate a ramp voltage whose gradient is linearly proportional to the number set into it. Hence its instantaneous value will be directly proportional to the product of the binary number and time elapsed. This device is also useful in graphics systems for vector generation.

2.5. GENERATORS

Character Generators

The most common and cheapest kind of character generator is the type using readily available MSI chips. In its simplest form it depends on a character format based on a 7×5 raster. Figure 2.3 shows typical characters of this form. The construction of these generators is based on a *read-only memory* (*ROM*). In a 7×5 matrix, horizontally scanned, each character has seven 5-bit registers allocated to it. Figure 2.4 shows the pin configuration of a commercial ROM.

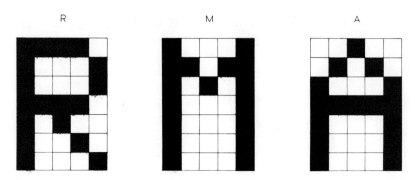

Figure 2.3. Typical 7 X 5 dot-matrix characters.

In order to operate the device a 6-bit character-code byte is applied to the "character-code" lines. This input causes the internal selection of the group of seven 5-bit registers corresponding to the coded character. The three "row select-address" inputs select which of the seven registers is presented to the output. Soon after this address number has been set five bits appear on the parallel outputs, corresponding to the pattern of that horizontal strip of the character. Thus, for the letter R shown, row-address lines 1 and 4 will give the output 1 1 1 1 0, row-address lines 2, 3, and 7 will give 1 0 0 0 1, row-address line 5 will give 1 0 1 0 0, and

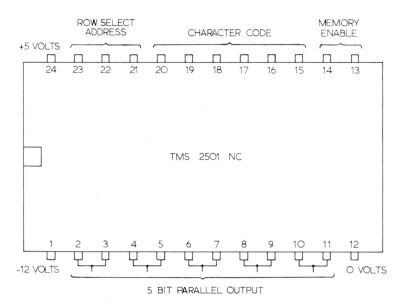

Figure 2.4. Pin configuration for a 7 X 5 dot-matrix character generator ROM.

row-address line 6 will give 1 0 0 1 0. If the device were to be designed to work in vertical scan mode there would be five sets of outputs, each of seven digits.

For TV-type raster scans the process of image generation is not difficult with this kind of device. A complete line of characters is written in seven adjacent horizontal sweeps. The binary character codes of the line to be written are fed to the generator, in turn, seven times over. The generator line address is incremented after each sweep. The process is a little more complicated if the TV scan is interlaced; in this case the line of characters will be written by four sweeps in the primary frame with odd-numbered line addresses, followed by three sweeps in the interlace frame with even-numbered line addresses.

These devices can be used with analog deflected displays. In this case it is a matter of convenience whether to use a vertical or horizontal scan system. The method of operation is to deflect the electron beam to the point where the corner of the character matrix is to be positioned. The x and y deflection voltages are then caused to scan the small area corresponding to the character matrix on the screen. The output of the generator is clocked out in synchronism with this scan and applied to the "Z mod", causing bright-up. There are various ways of generating the local scans. Normally it is most convenient to build simple counter and D-A converters in each coordinate as part of the character-generation circuitry. The voltages produced by these are added to the main x and y

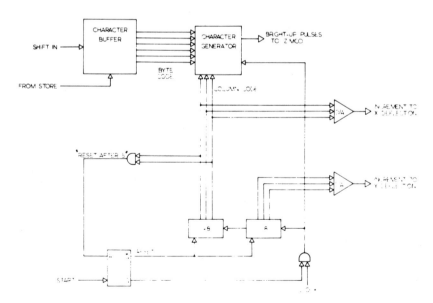

Figure 2.5. Character-generator logic.

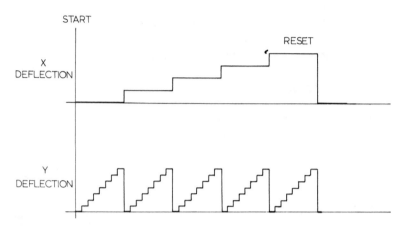

Figure 2.6. Character-generator scan waveforms.

deflection voltages in summing amplifiers. Figure 2.5 is a schematic diagram of a simple vertical-scan character-generator system. Figure 2.6 shows the x and y deflection waveforms during a single character scan.

A character byte is shifted into the character buffer, setting up the character code in the character generator. The generating logic is then triggered by setting the bistable which allows clock pulses into the system. The least significant three bits of the counter are D-A converted to generate a repeated staircase waveform to be added to the y-deflection voltage causing a vertical (column) sweep as the character generator puts out bright-up pulses where required. The most significant three bits of the counter are applied to a second 3-bit D-A converter, which produces a further staircase waveform to be added to the x deflection voltage, positioning the vertical sweeps in the horizontal direction. These three counter bits are also applied to the character-generator column select-address inputs. After the five columns have been scanned the system resets itself.

In order to energize sufficiently the phosphor of the CRT it is necessary to allow the beam to dwell on each spot for about $10\,\mu s$. In addition, at least $1\,\mu s$ delay is required to move to the next spot. Thus, to sweep the whole matrix can take up to $400\,\mu s$, plus the flyback times before each sweep. If the character is, say, a colon, it will only contain two dots which require bright-up. In order to gain speed it is an interesting and not difficult exercise in circuit design to arrange some feedback from the generator output to the controlling clock, giving 10-μs pulses where bright-up is required but allowing 1-μs pulses for scanning the zeros, thus making the best use of the logic speed of the MSI character-generator chip. In this way, the average scan of a character of about 18 dots (e.g., the R of Fig. 2.3) could take as little as $200\,\mu s$ to complete. Another useful variation when using this type of character generator in X-Y displays is to alter the scan voltage range and thus change the character size.

Better-quality characters can be produced by increasing the matrix size to, say, 10×8. This type of generator is usually accommodated on several standard chips or a larger-size encapsulation. The single MSI chip type of character generator has the advantage of being cheap, as it is manufactured by standard microcircuit techniques. Its disadvantages are that for some applications it is not fast enough and it is rather inflexible (i.e., the character set is restricted only to that which is available on the standard chip).

Prior to the availability of microcircuit character generators a type of generator based on a slave CRT was developed which functions on a similar principle. The small slave CRT has within it a target on which are deposited images of the character set formed in insulating material. A character to be written is selected by x and y deflection of the electron beam to the appropriate position on the target. The beam is then caused to sweep a raster over the deposited character. As the beam impinges on the deposited insulated sections of the raster the beam current is interrupted. On the main display the same raster is traced using the same deflection voltages. The interruptions of the beam current cause bright-up on the main display. thus drawing the character. This device is much more expensive than the microcircuit device and has now been supplanted by it.

Where maximum speed is essential (as in displays on which it is necessary to write many lines of alphanumeric characters) special devices must be used; the most notable of these is the *charactron*. This device is a special display CRT of considerable complexity. The electron beam is collimated to a narrow pencil and then directed at a stencil plate in which character shapes have been etched out. The beam is directed to the appropriate character by a preliminary deflection system. After passing through the plate the beam conforms, like an extrusion, to the selected character. It is then deflected once more onto the axis of the tube where it passes into the main x and y deflection system of the tube for positioning on the screen. It is not necessary to have much knowledge of electronics and CRT's to realize that the successful construction of such a tube is a feat of technology in itself and that it is not cheap. The cost of this kind of special device rules out its use in interactive graphics. It is, however, an important component in some high-speed photoprinters and similar devices which may be associated with interactive graphics systems.

Another well-established technique of character generation is to trace out the character with a set of short standard-length vectors which can be vertical, horizontal, or at $30°$ or $45°$ inclinations. Microprograms for each vector are built into hardware. Selection of a character calls a sequence of these microprograms. It is possible to design these devices to work at the maximum speed the tube deflection system and phosphor will allow. They are more expensive than the microcircuit matrix character generator when built of discrete components but they lend themselves to being designed also in MSI.

Function Generators

A common requirement for graphic displays is the drawing of straight lines, or *vectors*. A computer achieves this by generating constant-size increments of the x and y deflection values. This process is simple enough to program but it is usually advantageous to use a specially developed hardware function generator. Since this process corresponds exactly to the integration of a constant, the basis of vector generators is an integrator, either analog or digital. For generation of straight lines of arbitrary length, digital integration is ideal; suitable devices are manufactured as MSI microcircuits and commonly form the basis of vector generators in hardware display processors. For the vectors used in character generation mentioned earlier, however, the conventional analog integrator based on an operational amplifier is simpler and more effective. There is the problem, if these are used for larger vectors, of obtaining sufficient linearity and accuracy. The exact "address" of the end part of a digitally generated vector can be easily calculated, whereas this is not the case with the analog device owing to variation in amplifier gain and to drift. In order to determine the exact end-point position of an analog vector calls for the measurement of the x and y coordinates by A–D conversion. Then the vector generation would have to be controlled by a feedback system, which would add to complication and cost. For analytical curved-line generation, on the other hand, suitable voltages are easy to produce using analog integrators and these are commonly used where circles and ellipses are to be drawn at speed. It will be apparent that a suitable display processor for geometrical graphics of this kind is a small fast hybrid computer. These have been employed in some installations where the application warranted such an expensive provision. Nowadays an alternative to the analog computer in the hybrid system is the *digital differential analyzer,* or *DDA,* the main features of which are described in Chapter 3. This alternative has been rendered practicable by the development of suitable MSI components.

Although it is easy to see how versatile display processors can be built, capable of generating characters, vectors, and geometrically produced curves by hybrid computer techniques, these are not yet so commonplace that a "standard" configuration can be defined. There is still plenty of scope for system designers to explore the possibilities.

—

2.6. RASTER–TYPE DISPLAYS

Introduction

In a raster-type display the picture is drawn and regenerated by causing the electron beam to scan the display area on the tube face in a pattern of evenly spaced horizontal straight lines. During the time of one complete raster scan, or *frame*, the beam passes once through every point in the display. In order to produce an image, bright-up is caused at the appropriate instants within the scan time. The display data must therefore be programmed in serial form, with time as a coordinate, instead of the x and y position. This is the method by which television pictures are generated and refreshed. The rate of bit generation required for the display of a TV image has been discussed earlier in this text. For the time being a display to full TV standards is hardly practicable for general-purpose computer graphics. Nevertheless, the development of television makes available rather cheaply a range of display devices which have had the benefits of intensive research and large-quantity production. Naturally, computer graphics system designers have tried to make use of them.

Scan-Type Visual Display Units (VDU's)

Displays of geometrical and other two-dimensional images call for deflections of the CRT beam over arbitrary distances in any direction. An alphanumeric text display is sequential, character by character and line by line. For this reason most VDU's employ some kind of scan technique.

A simple VDU may be limited to 16 lines of text, each of 64 characters. If a character generator is used to produce the character images, then the total data-storage requirement for a serial store, with characters in the form of 8-bit bytes, amounts to $16 \times 64 \times 8$ bits, that is 8192 bits. At a refresh rate of 25 frames/s the serial bit frequency would need to be little more than 200 kbit/s. This pulse frequency is well within the range of the slowest and cheapest MOS shift-register device. Before the advent of MSI, VDU's commonly used an acoustic delay line as a serial store.

A sketch of a primitive VDU based on a recirculating store is shown in Fig. 2.7. The store consists of six 1024-bit MOS static shift registers; these are readily available and are not expensive. The deflection system is also simple; the horizontal deflection voltage is generated by an operational amplifier configured as an integrator. This is supplied with clock pulses causing it to generate a "staircase" voltage with steep ramps from step to step. The vertical deflection is controlled by a 4-bit D–A converter, giving 16 discrete levels corresponding to the text lines.

Characters are generated by an MSI ROM of the type described earlier using vertical scan. This system is sufficient to maintain an image of 16 lines

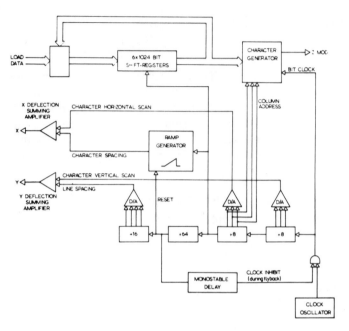

Figure 2.7. Schematic diagram of a scan-type VDU.

of 64 characters. Using static shift registers, the store circulation can be stopped and started to allow times for line and frame flyback, under the control of a monostable. The system is virtually asynchronous; the end of each line is detected to cause line flyback, while the end of the 16th line also causes frame flyback.

In order to generate the image in the first place, the circulating store must be loaded character by character. The data may be provided by a local keyboard or over the telegraph or telephone by an acoustic coupler. If the data is provided from a keyboard it will be in bit-parallel form, fit for immediate entry into the serializing buffer register. If the data arrives by line it will arrive in serial form at the pulse rate appropriate to the line. It must then be staticized and sent by parallel transfer to the buffer register. Today there is an MSI module known as the *universal asynchrnous receiver/trans-mitter* (*UART*) which performs this conversion. The UART is described in Appendix 1.

Codes and print formats for VDU's are expected to conform to those of a teletype or electric typewriter. The major problems that arise in using a circulatory store of the kind described above are due to its inflexibility. For the VDU to be convenient to use the operator needs to see where the current character is positioned. Hence he needs a cursor indication that he can see and move where he wants it. Facilities such as back space, erase, line feed up or down, and carriage return should be provided. These pose problems in synchronization for the logic designer.

Although the recirculating shift-register store is a cheap item, the principal disadvantage of a VDU of the type described above is that it fails to make use of most of the circuits provided in a television. It only employs the tube and the deflection yokes.

Recently developed VDU's employ TV monitors as the basis of their display. The cheapest TV displays are the standard broadcast receiving sets, which are manufactured in great numbers. Generally they are not so suitable for graphics use as are the monitors used for closed-circuit TV applications and the like. These are closely related to broadcast receivers but manufactured in smaller numbers. They cost more but are more suitable for adaptation, since they usually have no high-frequency tuning or audio system. The input is direct into the video stage and terminals are brought out allowing line- and frame-synchronizing pulses to be injected separately. In other respects monitors are little different from ordinary receivers.

The TV receiver or monitor is mass produced, and to make it economical it is designed solely for its purpose; little scope is allowed for adjustment, and modification is difficult and ill advised. Furthermore, many circuits and components are used for several purposes. A typical example is the considerable economy gained in generating the EHT voltage by applying the rapidly changing deflection current during flyback to a highly inductive winding. This produces peaks of several thousand volts which are tripled or quadrupled using diode and capacitor ladders. It is unwise to meddle with the scanning and flyback circuitry.

The scan and flyback control is based on multivibrator circuits which are set to "free wheel" at 1 or 2 frames/s less than the standard frame rate. The synchronizing pulses which cause flyback arrive to trigger the circuits just before their natural self-triggering would take place. It is therefore not possible to modify the frame rate by much, at the most about 2 frames/s either side of the standard rate. It is advisable to operate at exactly the standard rate, which is convenient since it is synchronous with the a.c. mains supply. The reason for this is that is is common practice to economize by not filtering out the a.c. mains ripple from the d.c. supplies but rather to use a "humdinger" which injects an equal and anti-phase mains ripple to cancel the effect. It is not important to know much about television techniques in order to use television devices for computer graphics; it is, however, sensible to refrain from pushing them beyond the bounds of their specification.

If a monitor is used as a display, the raster scan is completely provided and merely requires synchronization. All that needs to be provided to the monitor are signals into the video stage to cause bright-up and the synchronization pulses. Everything else required to generate the display must be done externally to the monitor at the correct frame rate.

A line scan has a duration of nearly 65 μs, of which the flyback occupies about 20%. Hence the duration of the visible line scan is about 48 μs. If the line is to hold 80 characters, each of 6 bits effective width, the access time of the horizontal-scan type of character generator needs to be about 600 ns; devices are available which are fast enough for this purpose. Storage devices, however, are more of a problem. One effective practice is to use six or eight MSI dynamic serial shift registers in parallel, 80 stages per line of text. This solution is reasonably satisfactory but it suffers from the same inflexibility as does the slower serial store mentioned earlier. Since the pulse rates are much faster, the logic design must also be more precise. Nowadays, designers tend to use *random access memory* (*RAM*) modules, fabricated in MSI, in configurations in which their speed is made adequate by organization. This has many advantages when it comes to providing operating facilities such as cursors and text editing. A useful feature is termed "roll round"; the text can be moved up or down the screen as though moved by the paper roller on a typewriter. Since the store is randomly accessed, the movement of a line merely means manipulation of the line address without any movement of the data itself. This "roll" facility is especially useful when the VDU is backed by a large store, such as that of a mainframe computer. An operator can "page through" many lines of stored data by continually operating the facility. For editing or searching through inventories, and similar tasks, this facility is quite efficient.

The speed at which data must be transmitted into a television output device, coupled with the amount of storage required to maintain a whole image, are still the main problems for designers who wish to utilize this kind of display. There are a number of techniques by which the problems may be rendered less severe.

Restriction of the display to alphanumeric information and the use of a fast character generator reduces both the speed and size requirements of the store required to support the image. A 7 X 5-matrix character generator emits 35 dots on the basis of only six input bits, giving nearly a six-fold saving in store size. If the text is in a fixed format, normally occupying only seven or eight horizontal sweeps out of each 16, a further two-fold saving is gained, making a total reduction in this respect of nearly twelve-fold. Further savings can be obtained by half-frame blanking or by using only one scan without interlace.

More sophisticated and expensive systems use character generators based on larger matrices, typically 10 X 8 or even 12 X 8. These allow a much larger character set to be used but require a larger byte for character selection and more logic to control them. Some generators have been designed to include in the character set symbols which can form parts of diagrams, and short vector sections which can be juxtaposed to form continuous lines, though restricted to a limited number of inclinations. A display of this kind is shown in Fig. 2.8. This display was generated on a Computek VDU (Computer and Systems Engineering Ltd., Rickmansworth, Herts, England: Computek 300 Graphics Terminal).

The use of specially designed character-generating devices, based on ROM's, allows satisfactory diagrams to be displayed so long as they are of a type where the diagram topology can be strictly formalized. Color monitors may also be used; the three color-gun controls are operated separately, and the resultant displays are not only pleasing to look at but can carry more information. Control and programming is necessarily more complicated but the results justify the extra expense.

Geometrical Graphics Displays using TV Monitors

The above discussion has centered on a display field of 500 to 600 by about 500 spots. If only 256 horizontal lines are used, without interlace, and with only 256 dots displayed per line, the number of spots required is reduced from about 250,000 to 65,536. If each dot is generated as a bit in a serial stream, then the bit rate in a horizontal scan can be calculated; 256 bits in 48 μs gives a rate of about 5×10^6 bit/s. Currently manufactured magnetic-

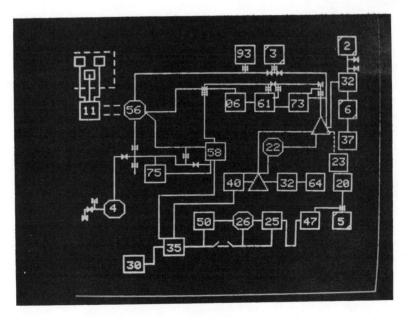

Figure 2.8. Display generated on Computek VDU.

disc stores operate at bit rates per track of between 2.5 and 3.5 Mbit/s. By using two tracks in parallel a rotating disc store is capable of generating a bit stream fast enough to maintain a TV-type display, and this technique has been used with notable success by the Data Disc Corporation (6). Many desirable features of pictures are difficult to achieve using scan-type displays. Other features are much easier to obtain with these than with X–Y devices. For instance, a continuous horizontal line is an easy figure to generate during a raster scan, and a continuous vertical line is not too difficult. An impressive display technique in the Data Disc system repertoire is the generation of histograms and filled-in rectangular areas, though this has little relevance to interactive graphics.

A feasibility study of the use of a conventional magnetic-drum store for controlling and refreshing TV displays was reported by Standeven *et al.* of Manchester University in 1968 (7). This study showed that, in the state of the art prevailing at that time, eight tracks could maintain a display. Progress towards successful TV-type displays using rotating stores has been dependent on the advances in magnetic-recording technology. Bit rates per track have increased and devices have become less costly. Experimental head-in-contact disc systems have been built with bit rates per track approaching 10 Mbit/s. Such discs, if they became commercially available, would be adequate to maintain a full standard display in pure black and white (i.e., without grey shades) on one track.

The technique for achieving full-capability graphic displays using TV scans is to generate each TV line as a group of computer or store words and then to serialize them as a continuous stream, in an analogous way to digital magnetic recording. The words are obtained from store by *direct memory access* (*DMA*), sometimes called *data break* or *cycle stealing*, as described in Chapter 4. Most modern computers, even small ones, are capable of emitting data by DMA at speeds which are greater than the required minimum. The problem with storing the display file in this form is size. If the image were to be continually refreshed from the computer, a large volume of store would be necessary and the computer's performance of other tasks would be greatly impaired. Off-loading the data onto a disc store and transferring the task of image regeneration allows the system to become more efficient. There remains the problem of mapping the display into serial form from the display file in the computer.

Writing onto a magnetic disc for graphic purposes has some significant differences from the conventional technique of digital data storage used in other computer applications. A vital requirement of computer-file storage is accuracy. Systems can only be run at speeds which give low error rates. For this reason most rotating stores use the form of recording in which each digit, 0 or 1, requires a complete cycle of an approximately sinusoidal waveform. It has long been customary with magnetic-tape systems to use more economical and compressed forms of modulation known as 'NRZ1" or "NRZ change". The basis of these two forms of modulation is that the polarity of the writing current, and consequent recording, is changed either to record each 1, or to record each change, from 1 to 0 or 0 to 1. In this way, each complete cycle of the recording waveform can, at maximum rate, carry the information of two digits; hence, each digit is represented by one reversal rather than one cycle. These modulation methods are inherently less reliable than the full-cycle recording, but they are faster (8). The accuracy requirements for a scan-type graphic display are orders of magnitude less than those required for digital data storage. A relatively large number of missing or redundant dots on a TV image makes little difference to the legibility of the image or even to its appearance. For this reason it is feasible to push the recording speed of a rotating store near to its working limits in graphical applications. On the other hand, there are phenomena of magnetic recording such as *crest displacement* (due to the magnetic fields of adjacent recorded digits) which are unimportant in digital data recording so long as they are not outside the limits of the data strobing, but in graphical work because the display is monitoring the data stream with a CRT, they may be visible and cause disagreeable distortion of vertical lines.

The Reading PICASSO System

This system, developed at Reading University in the UK, utilizes the fact that disc capability is currently adequate for a standard resolution display based on a matrix of 512×512 points. The British Standard for TV is for a 625-line display, of which 585 are available for use and not absorbed in the frame flyback. In order to obtain the required resolution, the displays must be operated in interlaced mode.

PICASSO is an acronym for "Pad Input to Computer and Scanned Screen Output", surely an appropriate name for a display system. The project has been financed by the Science Research Council of Great Britain; its aim has been to demonstrate the feasibility of a low-cost multiconsole interactive graphics system to make interactive graphics more easily available in educational, and similar, institutions.

The system is based on a magnetic disc unit manufactured by Process Peripherals Ltd. (Thatcham, Berks., England: Series 100 Disc Memories) who have experience in making disc units for television recording, for use in medical research, and similar activities. The disc used for the PICASSO project is digital; two tracks are devoted to each half-frame, making four tracks for each display. The current configuration, driven by a CTL Modular One computer (Computer Technology Ltd., Hemel Hempstead, Herts., England), maintains and controls five display consoles.

The disc is particularly suitable for use with TV displays as the disc speed of 50 rev/s is servo controlled. A disc driven directly from a synchronous motor would also rotate at 50 rev/s but there is a danger of it suffering from phase swing; that is, it may tend to oscillate about its exact in-phase position, causing the image to wobble. For an experimental system this is not acceptable.

Apart from its high resolution, the only technological innovation claimed for the PICASSO system is that it offers selective erasure and editing facilities, thus allowing interactive operation. This is achieved by maintaining a sixth set of four display tracks, that is, one more than the number of displays. The single clock track on the disc supplies the high-speed 10-MHz clock-pulse train for each display but the flyback synchronizing pulses and format waveforms are generated by logic associated with each display. The basic clock-pulse rate from the disc is 2.5 MHz, well within its capability. The 10-MHz rate is generated by a set of three delays within each clock-pulse time.

It is not possible to switch between reading and recording while "in sector", since this process occupies several microseconds. Thus changing the digital information in a display line entails reading the existing data off the disc, modifying the digit pattern, and writing the new data back onto the disc. The read-signal voltages are generated by flux changes detected by the magnetic read/write heads; hence the signal that is read is delayed by at least half a digit time compared with the reference clock. It cannot therefore be rewritten in the same clock-pulse time, that is, at the same position on the image. The storage requirement is too great to allow the whole image to be held in a buffer store or to be read back into the computer. For this reason, the image is rewritten onto the spare set of tracks as it is modified; the timing waveform of this set of tracks is delayed by the same amount as the reading and modification requires, thus retaining the relative addresses of the rewritten digits in the rewritten frame. This set of tracks is then monitored by the relevant display, and the old set of tracks becomes the spare set for the next modification process.

Although this system seems complicated it is economical. In earlier systems this kind of editing, where it has been provided, has been achieved by using a second disc unit as a buffer store. The hardware required amounts to little more than a set of binary counters deriving each display's synchronization pulses. At current logic prices this is not expensive. A hardware controller maintains the record of which tracks are associated with each display and organizes the appropriate changes when modification occurs.

The system embodies a conventional 7 X 5 dot-matrix MSI ROM character generator to write character symbols onto the disc; in the case of this simple character generator there is no significant cost gained by time-sharing it. If a more specialized device, or any complicated function-generating logic were embodied, then there would be an advantage in not having to provide such a device for every display. In fact, function generation, such as vector generation, is performed by software subroutines in the computer. The routine for drawing vectors is a fairly simple one due to the progressive nature of the scan which generates the image. An attractive feature of the system is that the computer need only draw and erase each vector once and can perform other work between these actions without having to refresh the image. Hence the overhead of computing required to generate functions is not important.

In the present configuration the computer must maintain a display file for each console. In the future the disc could store the display file, sending it back to the computer when required; one obstacle is that characters are held on the disc in decoded form, although the corresponding codes might be stored within the flyback periods.

The input device for PICASSO is worthy of note as it is so economical to implement. A resistive pad is used, similar to that described in the next section on input devices. This produces x and y voltage levels corresponding to the stylus position. The TV line- and field-scan ramp voltages are compared with the stylus x and y voltages, respectively. When coincidence of both coordinates occurs, a bright-up pulse is generated as a cursor. At the same instant the display-scan counters are sampled, giving the address of the cursor spot (expressed in line number and in position along the line) in digital form for transmission to the computer.

Before long, it is likely that fast logic will be cheap enough to provide a semiconductor register store for TV-type images at an economic price. In the meantime the PICASSO project has shown that significant economies can be gained by using TV techniques with a cluster of consoles, and that a range of interactive graphics activities is possible.

The MEMICON or LITHOCON

There is one device, the MEMICON (English Electric Valve Co., Chelmsford, Essex, England: MEMICON Electrical Storage Tube EP750) or LITHOCON (Princeton Electronic Products Inc., New Brunswick, N.J., USA: LITHOCON Electrical Storage Tube 1M800HS), which shows promise of being an ideal display store for use with TV output. It consists of a CRT which has a silicon wafer as a target for the beam. This target, about a square centimeter in area, has deposited on it by expitaxy a 1000×1000 matrix of bistable diodes. These diodes can be set to conduct or not to conduct, depending on the energy of the beam when it is focused on them. A lower-energy beam can be used to scan the array of diodes and the beam current then indicates their state. A stored pattern (generated either by a scan or by X–Y deflection) can be scanned off the target electrode and displayed repeatedly without degradation of the pattern. The principle of the device is reminiscent of the Williams Tube (9). A problem of implementing a satisfactory store with the device is that of generating sufficiently precise beam deflections. The deflection system must be (i) accurate to 1 part in 1000, (ii) fast, and (iii) able to cope with the deflection coils which are inductive. This is not a new problem but CRT system designers have not found it an easy one to solve.

2.7. INPUT DEVICES

Introduction

Interactive computer graphics consoles require at least one input device for use in conjunction with the display. Some kind of keyboard is normally needed so that alphanumeric information can be easily entered, but it is often necessary to have some means of transferring geometrical and topological information to the computer. There are a variety of methods which might achieve this. Before describing these it is as well to examine the requirements of such an input device; naturally, these depend on the application of the system.

A human with reasonable skill can draw to a precision of perhaps one-fiftieth of an inch. On an image area 10 in. square this represents a precision of 0.02 in 10, or 1 part in 500. Expressed digitally this requires 9 bits, which is well below the precision to which most computers work.

In some applications, graphical information which is entered into the computer can be described as "non-analytic". Typical of this type of information are contours on maps, shapes of coastlines, other geographical features, and experimentally determined curves such as ballistic trajectories. This kind of information is not suitable for transmission to a computer since it is in analog form. The input device must convert the data into digital form linearly and accurately. Since there are no formulae for generating such curves, the computer can do more than store the data as a series of points, each represented by one pair of coordinates. It is easy to fill a large store quickly with long strings of closely spaced points when the data is of this form. If this kind of work must be done, then there is a requirement for complicated and costly input-plotting devices and special operator skills. Such applications are, however, not the concern of this book.

The human tends to see things differently from the way the computer is best suited to handle them. For instance, most humans visualize triangles, quadrilaterals, or similar figures as areas bounded by lines which meet at corners. The computer is better suited to working in the fashion of coordinate geometry, storing a triangle as three points. It is this difference in the ways that machines and humans handle data that makes interactive graphics such a potentially powerful tool. A computer can easily generate a geometrical figure on a display for a human to look at. Let us suppose the problem is to determine whether a certain point is inside or outside the figure. The human can decide after a cursory visual inspection. For the computer to draw the same conclusion it needs to perform a series of tests and calculations. Typically, a human filter designer or servo designer can tell by the form of a curve or graph whether the device it represents has the desired qualities. It is often difficult to program the computer to judge by the same criteria. On the other hand, the computer can determine the distance between two points of which it holds the coordinates to the same precision as they are expressed (perhaps as many as 32 bits). The human, by visual inspection, rarely achieves a precision of better than 9 bits.

Bearing in mind considerations of the kind described above, it is now practicable to discuss the needs and capabilities of input devices and to study the details of some that are in current use.

The Light Pen

The position of honor must go on to the so-called *light pen,* not necessarily because it is the best device, but because it was the device chosen for use in the pioneer SKETCHPAD demonstration (10).

The light pen consists of a cylindrical pen-like holder, inside the barrel of which is a photosensitive device or *PE cell.* At the "writing" end of the pen is a small aperture, generally holding a lens which focuses any light at which the pen is pointed onto the PE cell. From the pen there is a cable which carries power to the PE cell and signals representing the light intensity back to the control electronics. When the pen is pointed at light of the right color and intensity, the control electronics generates a pulse or level which the computer can detect.

The operation of the light pen depends on the nature of the process of writing an image on the face of a CRT. If the pen is pointed at the screen and the spot which is generating the image passes through the visual field of the pen, then the PE cell is energized and a signal passes to the computer, generally causing an interrupt, that is, a jump from the current program into a special routine. The computer is generating the image on the CRT and it therefore "knows" what part of the image, and hence at what point on the screen, the current spot is being written. More accurately, when the computer is interrupted it goes into a search routine to determine which command the display processor was obeying when the interrupt occurred. From this it can determine the coordinates of the point on the screen at which the light pen is pointed. The field of vision of the light pen is wide compared with the size of a spot on the screen. This complicates the issue since the computer needs to determine not only when the spot becomes visible, but also when it is central in the light pen's field of view.

The description so far indicates the reason why the device was described as the "so-called" light pen; it does not write. The writing process must be done continuously by the computer. As a result of determining the position coordinates at which the pen is pointed, the computer may generate a spot, or more generally a small pattern, say a circle, a cross, or a Roman square. Once the pen reads a signal from a spot, the computer can generate another signal at that point. Superimposing the cursor figure on any point of the screen allows the pen to indicate a position to the computer as accurately as the human operator can place the cursor figure.

In order to draw on the screen, there must already be some image displayed there. Thus for drawing (as distinct from indicating) the technique is for the computer to generate at a convenient point on the screen a cursor figure which the operator can "pick up" with the pen. The form of the cursor figure is chosen by the programmer or systems designer to facilitate the "tracking" action. The cursor figure will cover a small area and take a finite time to generate. As the light pen detects it, the point of the figure which has been reached by the drawing process can be detected by the computer, indicating the point of the cursor on which the pen is positioned. Using this information, the tracking program moves the cursor so that its center is at that point. Thus when the pen is moved, the program detects the position error created and moves the cursor by servo action to follow it.

In addition to the position information derived from the pen, the computer needs control instructions: whether to draw lines, spots, or vectors; whether to erase data already on the spot indicated; in general, what to do at the indicated position. This information can be provided by switches (sometimes pedal operated) push buttons on the console, or a push button on the pen itself. A convenient technique, not yet commonly available, is a vocal command system, allowing the operator to give simple voice commands such as "erase", "stop", "draw", and the like. This is now possible and should be available soon if sufficient demand is created.

The light pen has a signficant advantage over other input devices in that its positional data is determined by the program and does not depend on any physical measurement of the actual pen position. The cursor is on the screen itself and can easily be aligned to any target image, to the limit of human accuracy.

Disadvantages of the light pen are that it is sensitive to ambient light and requires a bright moving spot on the CRT if it is to discriminate between wanted signals and reflections off the CRT face. If it is too sensitive it will pick up spurious signals. However, for comfortable viewing a CRT spot would not be very bright, not much brighter than the afterglow due to the screen-phosphor persistence. The sensitivity characteristics of PE cells are dependent on color, and some are fast and some slow. Thus a good system needs to compromise between spot brightness, phosphor color and persistence, cell sensitivity, and speed. Some humans have a far from steady hand and allowance must also be made for this.

The major disadvantage of a light pen is that it cannot be used conveniently with a storage-tube display because continuous refresh does not occur, and there is no bright spot once the image has been generated. This can be viewed as a disadvantage of either the storage tube (as indicated earlier) or the light pen. The two are simply incompatible.

The type of light pen described forms part of several commercial systems and is virtually the same as that used in the original SKETCHPAD demonstration. An alternative configuration was developed by Digital Equipment Corporation for use in systems like the PDP 15/76 on which the REDAC programs described earlier were implemented. The DEC light pen has no active element in the actual pen unit, merely a focusing system. Light picked up by the pen is transmitted by a fiber-optics cord into the main display unit and then applied to an electronic photomultiplier. The DEC GT40 System, described later, uses a photocell device of a more conventional kind. The PE cell is infrared sensitive and the CRT phosphor is doped to give a significantly improved infrared output. This seems a good solution to the problem of the writing spot being uncomfortably bright.

Tablets

Alternatives to the light pen are a range of devices in the form of writing tablets. In these a surface is provided remote from the CRT but corresponding to it. The user writes on this surface and the position of contact of the writing stylus with the surface is transmitted to the computer. Usually the computer is programmed to echo a dot or cursor on the display screen at the x and y coordinates of the stylus position. In interactive applications the operator generally watches the cursor rather than the stylus. Although there is only one commonly used output device for computer graphics, there are a variety of different devices for the simpler requirement of input. The reasons for this are several.

In the first place a designer, when confronted with a problem, is wise to look around to see if it has already been solved by somebody else. Techniques of moving a cursor image on a CRT screen have been widely used since the earliest days of radar, formerly to track targets for anti-aircraft weapons and nowadays for the more peaceful activity of air traffic control. For these purposes, experience showed that good devices were *joysticks* and *rolling-ball* transducers. The joystick or ball is mechanically coupled to the armatures of two potentiometers corresponding to the x and y directions; the voltage outputs are the analogs of the x and y coordinates. These can be supplied directly to the display to position the cursor; they can also be used by the tracking device, either in analog form or in digital form after A-D conversion. These devices can easily be coupled into a computer graphics system. However, they are not suited to computer graphics applications. The actions in aircraft tracking are those of following moving targets and the input device is often used to control the rate of movement of the cursor rather than its position. The actions of an interactive graphics operator are more directly connected with drawing than with tracking; a good test is for an operator to try and write his signature with either device. It can be done but it is awkward.

A second reason for the variety of input devices is that early designers thought it desirable to trace diagrams into a computer graphics system precisely and to scale. For work such as cartography this has its attractions, but for the reasons mentioned earlier it is not suitable for interactive graphics. The best tablet devices have an accuracy of about 1 part in 1000; it is difficult for a human operator to achieve such precision. A better way to apply this kind of input system is for the operator to enter the topology of the image into the graphics system in sketch form, and then to indicate to the computer the accurate coordinate values for the salient points of the image; this can be achieved via an alphanumeric keyboard. In this way the operator can obtain a visual impression of the image to a precision limited by the accuracy of his eyesight; the computer can perform the associated coordinate geometry to the full precision of its calculating powers. This is a sensible collaboration between man and machine. It is analogous to normal practice in engineering design; the engineer makes a sketch, marked with dimensions, but he draws only approximately to scale.

A third reason for the wide range of devices is that they are within the scope of the experimenter who is working with little support on a meager budget. Because the task is basically simple, a new idea can be implemented at little cost. It may be that to produce the same device as a commercial proposition is not so easy. The light pen illustrates this; it is only a few hours work to build a light pen out of "found-in-box" components and to make it work after a fashion. It is quite another problem to manufacture many of them to work in a wide range of conditions, under guarantee, for critical customers who require accurate and reliable operation.

The Rand Tablet

Hitherto the best known commercial tablet, the archetype of this kind of device, has been the *Rand* tablet (11).

The basis of this device is a wire grid of 1024 closely spaced wires in each of the x and y directions, encapsulated in a square plate. The wires are pressed in touch with a set of contact pads laid out in the margin of the square work area to provide a voltage driver. The pads are arranged in the traditional Gray-code pattern for 10 digits so that by energizing each of the 10 sets of pads in turn, each wire receives a unique pattern of pulses. This contact configuration is applied in each coordinate direction. The voltage pulses are sensed by a capacitive probe which reads the pattern of pulses from the wire nearest to it. Since the wires are energized in the Gray-code arrangement adjacent wires differ only by one digit. The Gray-code signals received by the probe are decoded into binary values. By subtracting each reading from the one before, the computer program can check for errors or pen lift-off; each signal should differ from the previous signal by 1 bit only. If the difference is more than 1 bit, the probe is assumed to have been lifted or there has been a read failure.

For a conveniently sized pad of about 10 in. square, the wires must be spaced about 0.01 in. apart. They must all make good contact with the supply pads. The width of the protective surface between the wires and the probe must be of the order of the wire spacing. This device requires great precision in manufacture and must be handled with care. Its only major drawback is the cost involved. It does, however, give a digital output and needs few external connections.

Other digital tablets have been designed but have had less commercial success than the Rand tablet. One such device uses two Mylar sheets on which conductors are deposited into closely spaced parallel grooves. The sheets are then juxtaposed with the grooves at right angles. Under light pressure there is no contact between the conductors in the two sheets. When a ball point or similar small-area contact is applied, the Mylar distorts sufficiently to allow a conductor in one orientation to make contact with one in the other, hence identifying a point in the matrix. This arrangement is difficult to decode; typically there are 1024 conductors in each orientation. It is as difficult to make as the Rand tablet and requires equally careful handling. Too great a pressure or too sharp a point can destroy the matrix.

All digital tablets have this same problem of decoding; the Rand-tablet decoding system is an elegant solution. On the other hand, digital tablets have the advantage of linearity and accuracy in their construction.

The Sylvania Tablet

The Sylvania tablet works on an analog principle (12). A conducting film is deposited on a sheet of glass. Two carrier waves are propagated into the conducting film, one in the x direction and the other in the y direction, at frequencies of 90 and 110 kHz. These carriers are modulated by a 1-kHz waveform. A probe placed in contact with the film picks up the two signals and separates them. They do not interact with each other since the components of the system are linear. Comparison of the phase of the demodulated 1-kHz signals with the master oscillator gives a measurement in the x and y directions of the distance of the probe from the line of propagation of the signal into the conducting film.

This system has a substantial advantage; the conducting film is transparent and hence the working surface is also transparent. It can be superimposed over a diagram for tracing, or it can be superimposed over the face of the display to act as a light pen. This latter application is full of snags owing to (i) the problems of indexing the CRT with the tablet, and (ii) optical problems caused by parallax. However, if tracing is demanded, this tablet provides a solution. The tablet itself need be neither costly nor fragile. At current prices, even the complicated electronics could be provided inexpensively, but, since the output is analog, A–D conversion is required.

In an attempt to obtain the best of both worlds, a tablet has been evolved which uses a coarse square grid of wires in a glass plate. The wires in each direction are fed from consecutive stages of two ring counters. The probe detects when the wires nearest to it are energized and stops corresponding binary counters which then register the coarse value of the coordinates in each direction. (Each enclosed square in the matrix has a side about 1 cm long.) The phase difference between the initial clock pulse and the detected pulse is then used to establish the fine position of the probe within the square.

This system possesses both the best and the worst features of the Rand and Sylvania tablets. The tablet is transparent, robust, and not difficult or costly to make. It does need A–D conversion and some complicated electronics on which its fine accuracy depends.

Resistive Film Tablets

In 1956 Bell Telephone Laboratories developed a tablet based on a conducting film bordered by resistors as an "electrographic writing device" (13). This preceded notions of computer graphics by some five years. The principle of this tablet can be seen with reference to Fig. 2.9. The resistors are stretched along the sides of the conducting film and joined at the corners A, B, C, and D. The linear resistance of these bounding resistors is low in comparison with the resistance per square of the conducting film. Let us suppose A and B are held at voltage V, and C and D at ground; owing to the high resistance of the conducting film, little current will flow through it and therefore there will be only a small voltage change along resistor AB which supplies this current. There will hence be an approximately rectilinear pattern of equipotentials and

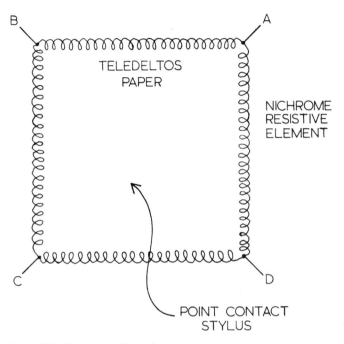

Figure 2.9. Simple resistive pad.

field lines in the resistive film between AB and CD. Since resistors BC and AD are linear there will be no voltage gradient between them and the resistive film. A probe sensing the voltage of points in the film will measure the analog of its vertical displacement from the edge CD. Let us suppose now A and D are held at voltage V, and B and C at ground. Similar conditions now apply across the resistive film and the probe will measure a voltage proportional to its displacement from the edge BC.

If A and C are maintained at V and zero volts, respectively, while B and D alternate in anti-phase between zero and V, the probe will read voltages in turn corresponding to x and y displacements on the tablet.

In 1965 Walker at Reading University developed a similar device for computer graphics use, unaware of the BTL development (14). The Reading device uses laboratory Teledeltos paper for the conducting film and nichrome electric-heating spirals for the bounding resistors in an effort to produce a really cheap input tablet. The nichrome spirals, being mass produced, are cheap and also adequately uniform; uniform linear resistors for laboratory use, being in quite small production, are not as cheap. A problem with this pad was found to be "pin-cushion" distortion; the equipotential lines, instead of being parallel, curve inwards towards the middle of each edge owing to the current that must flow towards the center of the resistor before flowing through the conductive film. The device developed at Reading overcame this entirely by curving the bounding resistors towards the center in a square-law shape. The principle of this correction is that the voltage drop along the resistor is compensated by the reduction of the path length through the Teledeltos paper. Figure 2.10 shows the arrangement. The Reading tablet has proved successful as a laboratory device, mainly because of its cheapness.

The Graf/Pen Data Tablet

An ingenious solution to the tablet input problem uses the technique of "hypersonic ranging" (Science Accessories Corporation, Southport, Conn., USA: Graf/Pen Sonic Digitizer). This tablet basically consists of a pair of linear microphones, each about 14 in. long, forming two sides of a square. These microphones detect acoustic signals from the stylus which, as well as being a ball-point device, embodies a tiny spark gap. The sound of the spark is detected by the microphones in each coordinate after a delay which is proportional to the distance between the stylus and microphone. Since the sound radiation is circular, the first sound detected by the microphone in each coordinate will give a true indication of the perpendicular distance traveled.

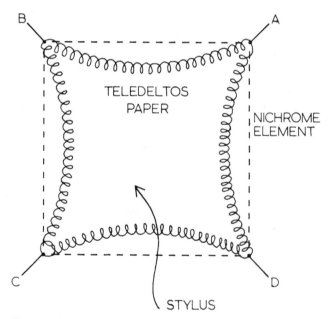

Figure 2.10. "Pin-cushion" compensated resistive pad.

This device has a number of obivous advantages. In the first place it can be laid on any flat surface or it need not be associated with a surface at all. Secondly, since the distance measurement depends on a linearly related time delay, a simple counter system can be used to measure the delay and hence distance, giving a digital value directly for transmission to the graphics control unit.

A fascinating possibility is that of using three linear microphones, suitably arrayed to allow three-dimensional operation. Alternatively the microphones could be made planar.

"Touch Wires" and Movable Cursors

All the input devices so far described are capable of drawing and writing as well as pointing. In interactive graphics, the ability to point to or indicate a section of the display screen is of prime importance; if drawing, as such, is not essential, then the pointing or indicating requirement can be simply met by a variety of other devices. Touch wires provide a good example. It is easy to design transistor circuits which will react to the contact of a human finger touching a wire connected to their inputs. A number of displays have been built with arrays of fine wires connected to touch-sensitive circuits stretched across the tube face. These wires may delineate or correspond to screen areas or they may have a code significance. The operator interacts with the display by touching the appropriate wire with a finger. Touch systems, wires, and contact pads need not necessarily be on the tube face; simple keyboard systems may also be constructed on the same principle.

Virtually all VDU's have some form of movable cursor spot brought out on the display, in an analogous manner to the cursor echoed onto the display by the more versatile pointing devices. Generally, on simple alphanumeric displays, the cursor is controlled by the line-feed and space-bar controls on the associated keyboard. In order to give more versatility some also have thumbwheel-controlled potentiometers allowing a fairly coarse adjustment of cursor position in a similar manner to joystick or tracker-ball inputs. Another alternative is to provide incrementing keys for up, down, left, and right movement of the cursor by fixed increments. This facility is further improved in some systems by making these keys respond to light or heavy pressure of the finger; a light touch gives one increment in the direction indicated, while heavier pressure causes the increment to be continuously repeated once or twice per second. This dual pressure effect may also be obtained by electronic timing; a single pressure causes a single increment, while continued pressure causes a train of increments.

Provisions of this kind cost little but have great value in the interactive process. There are many variations of them since they are almost trivial both in concept and implementation. Input devices for interactive graphics, as mentioned earlier, provide a fertile field for the ingenious and, doubtless, many more will be designed and tested as the ideas occur and the need arises.

2.8. THE GT40: A GRAPHIC DISPLAY TERMINAL

Introduction

This device, produced by the Digital Equipment Corporation, provides an example of a modern display terminal and a purpose-built display processor (Digital Equipment Corporation, Maynard, Mass., USA: GT40 Graphics Terminal). For several years DEC has been pre-eminent in the design and manufacture of small computers. They were among the first to manufacture and market computer graphics systems; they are also noteworthy in that they have always shown an appreciation of the poor man's needs and marketed many devices in the lowest price ranges. The GT40 terminal reflects their long experience in the field of computer graphics development.

The GT40 terminal consists of the following units: PDP 11/05 central processor unit (CPU and store); display processor unit; communications interface; keyboard unit; CRT display unit; light pen. Figure 2.11 shows the system arrangement. An important characteristic of the PDP 11 system is that it centers round a "Unibus"; this is a multichannel highway which interconnects the various parts of the system. The Unibus allows the CPU to communicate directly with all parts of the system; it also allows different parts of the system to become "bus master" and effect transfers of information to and from memory stores without the intervention of the CPU. These transfers are called "non-processor requests" or NPR's.

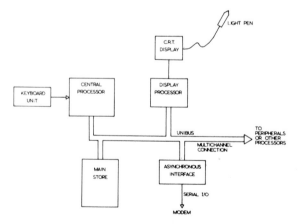

Figure 2.11. GT40 graphic display system.

The communications interface allows the system to be connected to other devices over telephone or telegraph channels in the range of permitted speeds.

The display processor is an autonomous unit having control of the CRT display and light pen. Once it has received an instruction to start it "runs" in a similar way to the central processor, obtaining instructions and data from the memory store of the PDP 11/05 using NPR's.

The display file is organized and maintained by the CPU, which interprets the graphics requirements of the source or object program. The CPU places the display file instructions and data in order in its memory store. In order to start display, the CPU transmits the address of the initial display instruction over the Unibus, causing it to be placed in the program counter of the display processor. The display processor performs the program from this instruction onwards until stopped by the CPU.

The display processor unit (DPU) contains four main registers: program counter; status register; X position (and graph plot increment); Y position (and character).

The function of the *program counter* is the same as in any computer processor; it contains the store address of the next instruction. It is incremented through the range of the memory addresses by the clocking system of the DPU, or it can be loaded to force "jumps".

The *status register* performs the functions of the order register in a conventional CPU. It receives instruction words and decodes them. Instructions may consist of up to three words, the second and third being data analogous to the "operands" of a conventional machine. The decoding of the *status word* (instruction) in the status register causes the successive calling in of data via the Unibus, and its disposal into the appropriate data registers, according to the function or "mode" setting in the status word. Although the CPU can monitor the contents of all four registers via the Unibus it can only transmit to the program counter.

There are two instruction sets: a set for control, and a set of mode instructions to organize the display processes. The set of control instructions are as follows: set graphic mode; jump; no-operation (no-op); load status register A or B. This set controls the cyclic operation of the DPU. "No-op" instructions have no effect and just replace unwanted instruction spaces in core. Load status instructions deal with facilities such as light-pen enable, "blink", and the fixed increments in graph plotting.

The set of graphic mode instructions consists of the following: vectors (long or short); point indication; character generation; graph plotting. The display graticule is to a resolution of 10 bits; about 1000 positions in each direction. Thus point-positioning and long-vector-generating instructions require the use of 10 bits in both data registers, and hence three NPR's. The remaining six bits in each register are used as identifiers and for bright-up information. Other instructions use a single 16-bit data word, requiring only two NPR's.

Inplementation of the Display Functions in the GT40 Display Processor

Point Mode. The x- and y-deflection voltages are supplied to the CRT by summing amplifiers as shown in Figure 2.12. The inputs to these amplifiers are from the various function-generating devices. The most direct function is point mode. The x and y coordinates in the data registers are transferred to two 10-bit registers called X and Y position-hold registers. The output of these two registers form the inputs to ladder-type D-A converters; the analog output voltages are applied to the deflection-summing amplifiers. The maximum settling time for the CRT yoke current drives is 21 μs; if the point is to be displayed, a bright-up pulse is given after this period. This basic function of beam positioning is also used, without bright-up, as the initial positioning instruction in vector or character generation.

Graphplot. The implementation of this mode takes account of the fact that in normal graph plotting only one coordinate (the ordinate) takes an arbitrary value, the other (the abscissa) advancing by standard increments. One

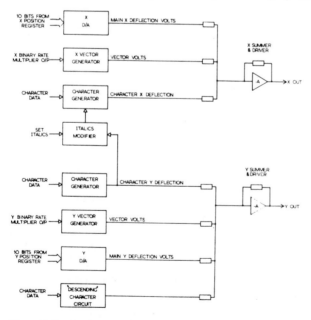

Figure 2.12. Analog x- and y-deflection drive arrangement.

of the load status instructions sets the increment for the x or y abscissa when graphplot mode is called. The ordinate values, called successively from the CPU store into the data register, are D-A converted and displayed. This technique of graph plotting has obvious advantages of speed and simplicity over the method specifying each point completely in absolute terms.

Character Mode. Since the data registers are of 16-bit length, two 8-bit character bytes can be held in one data register; this allows the normal form of character output to be in pairs. The character generator is based on a ROM giving an 8×6 dot character matrix in vertical-scan mode (as described earlier). In order to give maximum speed the scan is bidirectional; the character is commenced in the left-hand bottom corner, scanned upwards for the first column, downwards for the second, up for the third, and so on. An ingenious modification of the scan-voltage waveform allows the columns to be inclined giving the effect of italics, if called for by the presence of a bit in the status word. Figure 2.13 shows how simply this is achieved. The character vertical (column) deflection voltage, applied to the y deflection amplifier, is the triangular waveform (Fig. 2.13a); it is used in both normal and italic symbol generation. The horizontal increments for normal symbol generation are provided by the staircase waveform (Fig. 2.13b), which steps the generation column by column. In order to generate italic characters the two waveforms are added in a simple circuit to produce the waveform shown in Fig. 2.13c which gives x increments which slant the vertical scan as shown in Fig. 2.13d.

The character set consists of 96 ASCII symbols together with 31 special patterns for Greek letters, mathematical symbols, etc. It was stressed earlier

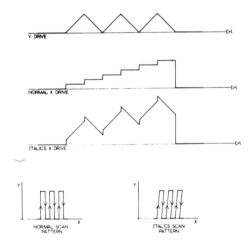

Figure 2.13. Generation of italics deflection waveforms: (a) y driving voltage; (b) normal x driving voltage; (c) italics x driving voltage; (d) x–y scans.

that it is important to make a graphics display pleasing to the eye. The five lower-case characters j, g, p, q, and y are "descending" in the sense that their tails go below the base lines of the text. Special circuitry is included to shift these letters down by the required amount. Lower-case letter components do not normally occupy positions in the first of the six columns of the character matrix. The presence of these five letters is indicated to the display circuitry by a dot in the first column; the detection of this dot in a lower-case code causes the downward shift of the beam during the generation of the character. The bright-up is suppressed, blanking this indicator dot. It is arguable whether or not this shift gives any improvements in legibility, but it does give the text a more pleasing and normal appearance and it has been judged by the device designers to be worthwhile. Both this and the italics facility illustrate how ingenuity can be used to improve presentation.

Vector Modes. The vector-drawing technique of the GT40 display processor makes use of hybrid circuits, and provides an illustration of a happy combination of analog and digital devices. There are two vector modes, long and short; they differ only in that for short vectors one data word is sufficient to hold both x and y increments, whereas long vectors are defined by two 10-bit numbers requiring the transfer of two data words.

The first function in the execution of a vector instruction is in point mode to establish the vector start point; this sets up the x and y coordinates in the holding registers where they are converted by the D–A converters and applied to the x and y deflection amplifiers to position the beam. The horizontal and vertical displacements ΔX and ΔY are transferred from memory into the data registers. In the first place the ΔX and ΔY values are used to derive the gradient for drawing the vector. They also provide information which terminates the drawing process when the vector is complete.

In order to generate the two ramp functions of the x and y deflection, voltages which will cause the electron beam to trace out the vector, ΔX, and ΔY are each applied to a 10-bit binary rate multiplier (BRM). The outputs from these BRM's are trains of pulses of frequency proportional to ΔX and ΔY. When these two pulse trains are fed to integrating amplifiers, the amplifier outputs are voltage ramps whose gradients are also proportional to the values of ΔX and ΔY, and therefore in the ratio of ΔX to ΔY. These ramp voltages are added to the x and y initial deflection voltages in the deflection-summing amplifiers, causing the beam to deflect along the line of the wanted vector.

The larger of ΔX or ΔY is also loaded into a counter, the down-count register. As the vector is generated, this counter is decremented by clock pulses; when it reaches zero, the vector process is terminated since the whole of the Δ increment has been traversed. At the same time, the X and Y position data registers are either incremented or decremented, according to the vector direction, by the x and y count pulses. Thus at any instant during the generation of the vector, the x and y values of its current end-point are available for inspection by the CPU, since these registers can be monitored as mentioned earlier. This arrangement allows the CPU to coordinate the current vector end-point with a light pen "hit".

When the down-count register becomes zero and stops the generation, the X and Y position register contents are shifted into the X and Y hold registers so that they may be used as the start point of a succeeding vector.

The pulse-rate output of the BRM is proportional to the magnitude of the number set into it. If small values of ΔX and ΔY are used, the output rate will be small also and the vector will be drawn slowly. In order to obviate this, before the vector-generation process is started, the ΔX and ΔY register contents are normalized by left-shifting them in their registers until the larger one has a 1 in the most significant digit position. The two registers will then contain the largest values of ΔX and ΔY which are in the correct ratio to define the vector gradient. This process ensures that vectors will be generated at maximum speed regardless of length.

Point Relative. In order to draw graphs with points at arbitrary distances in both coordinates a further function is provided based on the short vector mode. In this case the x and y relative displacements are entered into the data register in the same way as ΔX and ΔY for short vectors, and the new x and y values are arrived at as in a vector but no bright-up is generated for intermediate positions. This technique has the advantage over graph plotting by point mode in that only one data word is needed for each point instead of two.

The Display File for the GT40 Graphics System

It was stressed earlier that an essential requirement for an efficient image-regeneration system is to keep the display file simple and concise, so that regeneration requires as few store accesses as possible and the display program occupies a minimum of storage. The use of the display processor unit does much to achieve this. The following is a typical program sequence.

Long vector:	Set graphic mode instruction (point mode)	These three words establish the start point
	X Y two point data words	
	Set graphic mode instruction (long vector)	These three words determine the vector
	ΔX ΔY two long-vector data words	

The first long-vector data word, in addition to ΔX, carries the bright-up instruction and vector-direction data. The vector is drawn on receipt of the second word. If two more data words immediately follow in the next store locations, a second vector is drawn, concatenated with the first. Thus only 10 store words are needed to position and draw a triangle; if the figure were a small one, consisting of three short vectors, seven words would suffice.

Setting up a line of text is also an economical process. As for the vector above, the first three store accesses are to establish the start point. The next instruction would then be to set character mode and after that each data word brought from store would cause two characters to be displayed. The next character positioning is automatic after each character is displayed. Thus a line of 80 characters requires 44 store words to be accessed. Because direct memory access is used this is considerably faster than a conventional VDU. It is arguable whether the storage requirement is reduced.

As we shall see later. The GT40 uses a relatively simple display processor. In Chapter 3, the operations of translation, scaling, and rotation of input data are described. These are important as far as the user is concerned. Because points and vectors can be defined relative to the current spot position in the GT40 a symbol defined entirely in this fashion can be positioned at any point on the screen. Hence translation is possible, but no facilities for the other two operations are available. Rotation is particularly difficult and expensive to achieve, and scaling often costs more than it is worth.

One programming facility which is not provided by the GT40 is subroutine entry and exit (although simple jumps are allowed). Subroutines allow a symbol to be defined once as a set of instructions, and these can then be called many times at different places. The advantages of this are apparent from the discussion in Chapter 3. However, the GT40 does provide a useful alternative in the set status command which causes the DPU to stop display and interrupt the CPU. Since the CPU can read all the display registers, it can now emulate the action of a subroutine call. This is helpful because the programmer can specify any kind of action and is not restricted to a fixed type of subroutine call. This allows the programmer flexibility in structuring the display file.

It is customary to end a chapter with a conclusion. In the case of this chapter on graphical hardware, the best conclusion is probably the DEC GT40 itself. It embodies much of what has been discussed in a harmonious whole, and with all the necessary choices taken and compromises made. It does not do everything, but it is not a costly device. It has a typical good display, and a typical light-pen and keyboard input. The choice of phosphor has been made as a sensible compromise between the optical requirements of the human and the light pen. The system is flexible, can regenerate its own images, is easy to program, and the storage requirement is economical.

In the design of the display logic, the designers have arrived at a useful mixture of analog and digital techniques, giving a reasonable set of function generators and yet being economical in electronic hardware. Finally, the designers have attended elegantly to the cosmetic aspects of the display with "descending" characters and the generation of a kind of italics. The latter, although cosmetic, virtually doubles the character set for the extra cost of a handful of resistors and transistors.

The object of this chapter was to bring attention to the range of devices available to the designer and to point out their merits and demerits and the circumstances in which they apply. There can be no unique "right" solution, but merely what seems to be the best compromise, in the circumstances, which meets as many of the requirements as is reasonable. The DEC designers, with much experience and wisdom, have done just that. There is scope for other equally "correct" designs to meet the same, and other, specified requirements. Perhaps this chapter will help to stimulate their development.

REFERENCES

1. Poole, H. H. *Fundamentals of Display Systems.* Spartan Books, Baltimore, Md., 1966.
2. Popplebaum, W. J. *Computer Hardware Theory.* Macmillan, London, 1972.
3. Hankins, H. C. A., and Hughes, G. The application of cathodochromic displays to interactive computer graphics. *Brit. Comp. Soc. Comp. Bull.* 16(9), 440, Sept. 1972.
4. Gordon, B. M. Effects of noise on A/D conversion accuracy. *Comptes Rendus des Journees d'Electronique Conversion A/D et D/A, Ecole Polytechnique Federale de Lausanne, Lausanne, Switzerland, Oct. 1973.*
5. Analog Devices Incorporated, Norwood, Mass. *Analog–Digital Conversion Handbook,* 1972.
6. Lovercheck, L. R. Raster scan technique for multicolour graphics displays. *Electronics,* **41**, 111, 5 June 1972.
7. Standeven, J., Mikailovic, S., and Edwards, D. B. G. Multi-console computer display system utilising television techniques. *Proc. IEE* **115**(10), Oct. 1968.
8. Hoagland, A. S. *Digital Magnetic Recording.* John Wiley, New York, 1963.
9. Williams, F. C., and Kilburn, T. A storage system for use with binary digital computing machines. *Proc. IEE* **96**(3), 81, 1949.
10. Sutherland, I. E. SKETCHPAD: A man–machine graphical communication system. *Proc. SJCC 1963,* p. 329. Spartan Books, Baltimore, Md.
11. David, M. R., and Ellis, T. O. The Rand Tablet: A man–machine graphical communication device. *Proc. FJCC 1964,* p. 325. Spartan Books, Baltimore, Md.
12. Texeira, J. F., and Sallen, R. P. The Sylvania Tablet: a new approach to graphic data input. *Proc. SJCC 1968,* p. 315. Thompson Books, Washington, D.C.
13. Bell Telephone Laboratories. *Electrographic Transmitter.* U.S. Patent No. 2925467, 1960.
14. National Research and Development Corporation (UK). *Electrographic Writing Apparatus.* UK Patent No. 1267699, March 1972.

Software for Interactive Computer Graphics

3.1. INTRODUCTION

The previous chapter studied the hardware elements of interactive computer graphics systems in relation to the user's requirements as discussed in Chapter 1. In this chapter we look at the software elements of these systems in relation to the applications in which they are used. The chapter commences with an overall description of the graphics system, followed in § 3.2 by a more detailed description of the individual elements of the system. Within these descriptions other ideas are introduced which are not immediately involved with the graphics system; these are discussed in § 3.3.

Some confusion may arise from the treatment of graphical structures and data structures. An explanatory note is appropriate. Although these two structures could be related in a system, they are logically distinct. Unfortunately the situation can become confused because the same entity is often used for both. In this chapter graphical structures are presented separately from data structures to try and avoid the confusion.

The Graphics System

The part played by graphics in a totally computing system is one of input–output, and interactive graphics means input–output of a real-time conversational nature. The design of the graphical part of a system depends ultimately on the input–output requirements of the applications program. Some systems have no application apart from being automated drawing aids, but usually the graphics is subordinate to the application. Nevertheless graphics is important because it forms the interface between user and applications program, and its design affects the appearance of the whole system.

Graphics has its main impact as an output device. This is because the human brain is a very adept processor of visual information; it is so adept, in fact, that graphical input can be accomplished successfully only by repeating the input on the output channel. The user can then perceive visually the effects of the input.

Graphical input starts at the display. By some means a point on the display is indicated, and the problem is to relate this point to the structure it represents in the applications program. There are two ways of doing this. The more common method is to repeat the process of outputting the picture from the applications program until a display point is produced that is near enough to the input to register as a "hit". The structure in the applications program currently acting as source is then known to be the one indicated by the graphical input. The other method involves associating with each instruction given to the display hardware information indicating the originating structure in the application program. This auxiliary information can be stored and ordered in a way simply related to the display coordinates. A graphical input (which is expressed in display coordinates) can then be related back to the applications structure.

The prime function of graphics software is to transfer data between the applications program and the display hardware. The applications program may output data by issuing commands or by creating some sort of data structure. In either case, the output relates to the application rather than to the final picture on the display. For example, an electronic analysis program may use graphics to build up a picture of the circuit to be analyzed. The picture displayed is composed of connected electronic symbols. The applications program is concerned only with the connections between components and the values of the components, whereas the graphics is concerned mainly with the position of the symbols on the screen, and their shape, size, and orientation.

The applications-dependent part of the graphics software accepts commands from the applications program, or scans a data structure produced by the applications program and generates a description in two-dimensional space. This may involve very little processing; for example, the control-system analysis program described in Chapter 1 produces x, y coordinates directly and needs only axes and some annotation to be added. Applications like the electronic-circuit example require a more complicated treatment. The symbols from which the diagram is composed are few in kind, but repeated often. The applications program specifies the kind of symbol and the points to which it is connected. The graphics program has to generate the shape for each component in the right place and in the right orientation. In order to do this it uses a master copy of the shape of each component, which is rotated to the right orientation and then shifted to the right position in the two-dimensional field.

The display-dependent part of the graphics software has to manipulate the two-dimensional field to a form suitable for the display hardware. Conceptually, the field extends to infinity in all directions, but practically it is limited by the size and range of the number representation. The display hardware is typically even more limited, and usually uses integer cartesian coordinates of a relatively small range (say 0–4096). The display hardware has a rather coarse view of a small part of the field, which consequently must be increased or decreased in scale and then translated in position to bring the area of interest within the capabilities of the hardware. Material lying outside this range must be clipped off. The remaining data can then be translated into instructions driving the display.

The simplest and probably the cheapest form of display is the point-positioning display, where the computer uses digital-to-analog converters to drive the x and y axes and the intensity of a cathode-ray tube. In order to display a picture the computer calculates and outputs each point. This can give great flexibility and economy of storage, but is very slow. Moreover, to avoid flicker the picture has to be redisplayed continually and this places a heavy load on the processor. A storage tube can hold a picture without the need to refresh, but an erasure of any part of the picture involves erasing everything (a relatively lengthy process) and rewriting the modified picture. This precludes displays involving continuous movement, essential for tracking an input. In order to speed the output process, character generators and vector generators are used which reduce but do not eliminate the load on the processor. Processor loading is removed altogether by the *display processor*, which takes its display instructions directly from the main computer store without the intervention of the main processor. The main processor usually has access to registers in the display processor so that is can determine the current state of the display; this is necessary when tracking an input.

The data paths through a graphics system are shown in Fig. 3.1. The diagram is general and contains elements which may not be present in all systems.

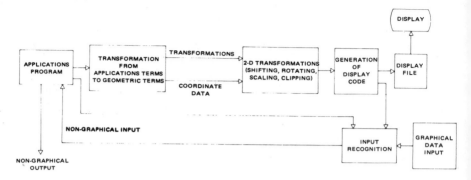

Figure 3.1. Data paths through a graphics system.

3.2. ELEMENTS OF THE SOFTWARE SYSTEM

The Applications Program

The applications program specifies what is to be displayed. It may do this by issuing definite commands or by building a data structure which represents the picture. In the latter case a separate process scans the data structure and generates the picture. The degree of structuring used by the applications program to describe the picture depends purely on the application itself. The picture may have no particular structure, in which case it is best described in terms of point coordinates. Examples of this sort of problem include processing of car-body shapes, contour lines, and graph plotting. Most pictures, however, have a definite structure. Points and lines which represent a separate object, for example, are more closely associated than other points and lines in the display. Within an object, points and lines sharing common coordinates have a closer association than other points and lines of the same object. The disposition of the objects themselves may be structured, as when characters are grouped into words or when electronic symbols are linked together in a circuit. When such a structuring exists, the applications program usually deals with units of the structure and will describe the display in the same terms. This requires the display description to be structured in the same way.

The most common way of structuring the points and lines in a display is to associate them into sets. The applications program then deals, not with points and lines, but with sets; when a transformation (such as a shift, rotation, or scaling) is applied to a set, it is applied by implication to all the points and lines which make up the set. At higher levels the sets may be associated to produce subpictures, frames, circuits, and maps. The way in which these structures are built up depends entirely upon the application.

Display Procedures

If the applications program generates the picture by issuing specific display commands, it can build up the desired structure by means of nested *display procedures* (subroutines) (15). Let us suppose the function of a program is to analyze circuits containing resistors and capacitors. The program will contain a procedure called **CAPACITOR** which draws a horizontal capacitor at the origin, and a similar procedure called **RESISTOR** which draws a resistor. The procedures will define their objects in terms of the coordinates of the end-points of the lines from which they are made. The definition will depend on the facilities of the language in which the applications program is written, as in the following hypothetical example.

```
DEFINE RESISTOR
   LINE FROM (0, 0) TO (20, 0) TO (30, −10) TO (50, 10) TO (70, −10)
      TO (90, 10) TO (100, 0) TO (120, 0)
END RESISTOR

DEFINE CAPACITOR
   LINE FROM (0, 0) TO (50, 0)
   LINE FROM (50, 20) TO (50, −20)
   LINE FROM (70, 20) TO (70, −20)
   LINE FROM (70, 0) TO (120, 0)
END CAPACITOR
```

If executed, these procedures would produce the displays shown in Figs. 3.2 and 3.3. Figure 3.4 shows (on the same scale) the result of a similar CIRCLE procedure.

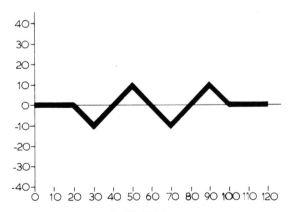

Figure 3.2. Display of RESISTOR.

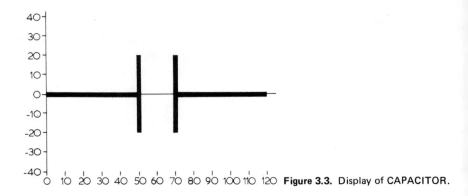

Figure 3.3. Display of CAPACITOR.

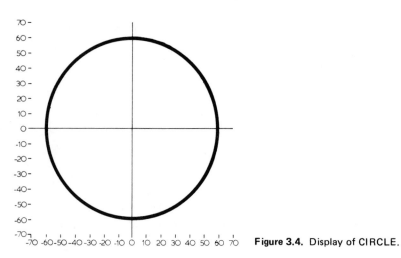

Figure 3.4. Display of CIRCLE.

In order to define a higher entity, say a filter which includes instances of resistors and capacitors, a new procedure is defined which calls the RESISTOR and CAPACITOR procedures as it needs them.

```
DEFINE FILTA
   CAPACITOR AT (0, 120)
   CAPACITOR AT (120, 120)
   RESISTOR ROTATED (PI/2) AT (120, 0)
   LINE FROM (0, 0) TO (240, 0)
   CIRCLE SCALE (0.1) AT (0, 120)
   CIRCLE SCALE (0.1) AT (0, 0)
   CIRCLE SCALE (0.1) AT (240, 120)
   CIRCLE SCALE (0.1) AT (240, 0)
END FILTA
```

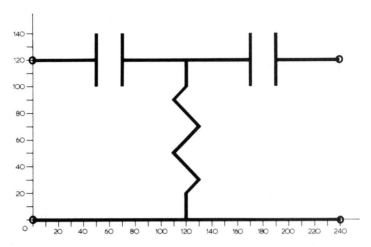

Figure 3.5. Display from FILTA procedure.

Execution of the FILTA procedure gives the display shown in Fig. 3.5. The FILTA procedure can then be called in different positions to build up a larger circuit.

A display procedure call is generally accompanied by additional commands which apply two-dimensional transformations to the whole process. For example, the FILTA procedure copies the capacitors from the region around the origin (where the master copy is defined) to the top of the diagram; it copies the resistor, rotated from horizontal to vertical, and then moves it to a position between the two capacitors; it makes scaled-down copies of the circle and places them at the filter terminals.

Another transformation commonly used is to mask off all material lying outside a defined area. Although the area can have any shape, a rectangle with sides parallel to the axes is invariably used for computational simplicity. An example of its use in the hypothetical applications program would be

FILTA WITHIN (0, 0, 150, 140).

The WITHIN element specifies the opposite corners of the rectangle through which the filter is seen. The result is shown in Fig. 3.6.

It is useful to be able to define a mapping from one (rectangular) region onto another. This is equivalent to a scaling and a translation. The statement

FILTA WITHIN (0, 0, 150, 140) ONTO (10, 10, 20, 20)

puts a diminished version of Fig. 3.6 into the square which has opposite corners at (10, 10) and (20, 20). The result is slightly distorted as the source area is not square. A statement like

RESISTOR ONTO (10, 10, 20, 20)

puts a *complete* resistor into the square bounded by (10, 10, 20, 20). Since the master copy of the resistor is not square the result will also be distorted.

The use of nested display procedures to structure a picture gives great flexibility in the representation of the picture. This is because the display procedures can use the general-purpose features of a programming language, in particular the conditional execution of statements. Alternative representations for a structural unit can be selected by conditions in the applications program. For example, let us suppose that an alternative representation of the filter is block form shown in Fig. 3.7, and that this representation is generated by a display procedure called FILTB. A new procedure can be defined which selects one of these representations according to some global condition. Let us suppose we wish filters to be represented by FILTA if a global variable *blockdiagram* is false, and by FILTB if *blockdiagram* is true. This would be written as follows in our hypothetical programming language.

DEFINE FILTER
IF BLOCKDIAGRAM THEN FILTB ELSE FILTA
END FILTER

In the same way it is easy to create procedures for other tasks demanding flexibility, such as elimination of detail at small scales.

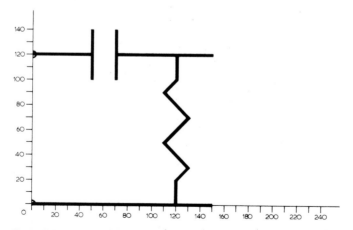

Figure 3.6. Display of FILTA WITHIN (0, 0; 150, 140).

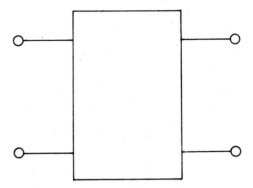

Figure 3.7. Block representation of a filter.

A picture is caused to be displayed by executing the procedures which define it. As higher-order procedures activate the lower-order ones nested inside them, the structure is unravelled into a linear list of coordinates. The transformations are collected separately from the positional data. Both are sent to the transformational routines where any scaling, shifting, rotating, or clipping is done. The transformed coordinates are then compiled into instructions which can drive the display, and placed into the display file. The overall data flow is shown in Fig. 3.1.

In an interactive environment, the user will manipulate the display by moving small objects about and altering the picture gradually. When a change is made, most of the displayed picture will remain unchanged. Moreover, the alteration must be fast, especially if the illusion of motion is required. There must be some way of avoiding the re-execution of the whole display program to effect only a small change in the display. This can be achieved by regarding the display as being built up from superimposed *frames*. Each frame is represented by a *frame procedure,* which calls the appropriate display procedures needed to make up the frame. Each frame procedure is allocated a separate segment of the display file. The frame procedures can then be re-executed independently of each other. Safeguards must exist in the graphics system to take corrective action when a frame procedure produces too much display code to fit into its allocated display-file segment.

The hypothetical language used in these examples is a general-purpose programming language extended (by display procedures, transformation commands, etc.) to deal with graphics. As presented here, the extensions are unlikely to be accommodated without modification of the language compiler. A more common approach is to provide a package of procedures or subroutines defined within the terms of the parent language; it is probably fair to say that a graphical subroutine package always gives a more obscure and unreadable program than a language extension.

Graphical Structures

An alternative way of handling graphical entities is to represent them by data structures rather than by procedures. The difference to the applications programmer is that he builds the graphical structures using the data-handling facilities of the programming language, rather than by using nested procedures. The most suitable method depends on the language facilities, and ultimately on individual taste. The commands used to build the graphical structure may in fact closely resemble the display procedures illustrated in the last section. One way of representing a graphical structure is shown in Fig. 3.8 where a lattice structure is used to represent FILTA. Once such a structure is established it acts as a description of the displayed material, and can be interrogated and manipulated by the applications program. However, manipulations like that used in the FILTER procedure, which selects one of two possible ways of displaying a filter according to the state of the applications program, are awkward to implement on a structure as shown in Fig. 3.8.

The applications program displays the graphical structure by calling a system-display routine which scans the structure. Usually, the start point of the scan can be specified, so that if desired a picture can be generated from a part of the complete structure. The scanning routine is performed in a way analogous to the execution of the display procedures. It traces its way through the graphical structure, expanding the subpicture and definitions into their constituents and finally into a linear list of display coordinates. Positional data and transformational data are collected separately, sent to the transformational routines, compiled into display processor instructions, and entered into the display file. The overall data flow is shown in Fig. 3.9.

In some circumstances the scanning routine can optimize the use of the display file. Some display processors have subroutine facilities, and a subroutine call is equivalent to a pointer to a subpicture. A display processor with subroutine capability would therefore be able to trace its way through the structure of Fig. 3.8, although it is unlikely to be able to cope with the scaling and rotation transformations. In pictures or parts of pictures which are unmodified by scaling or rotation, the structuring can be preserved when producing the display-file code. If a symbol is scaled or rotated, then the scanning program transmits the transformed coordinates in full to the display file; otherwise the display file receives only a subroutine call to the master symbol definition. This can substantially reduce the size of the display file.

Graphical Structures as Data Bases

The graphical structure shown in Fig. 3.8 carries more information than that

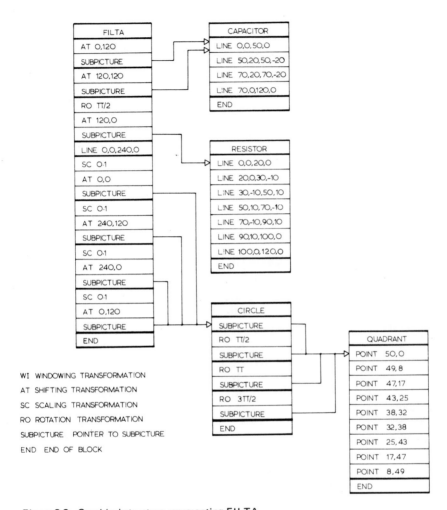

Figure 3.8. Graphical structure representing FILTA.

required just to define the picture. In addition, each block carries the name of the symbol it represents. Thus, the block of commands defining the filter is headed by a cell containing the characters FILTA, the resistor block is headed by **RESISTOR**, and so on. The character strings are never encountered by the scanning routine and play no part in defining the picture. They have meaning and usefulness only to the applications program. The non-display part of the structure can be expanded in a variety of ways to carry other sorts of non-graphical information, for example the value of each component, its cost, and what other components connect with it. Such a structure acts both as a

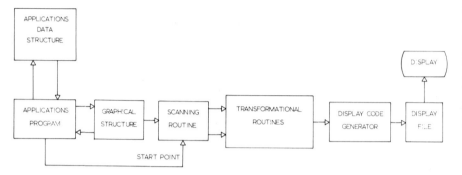

Figure 3.9. Graphics system using a graphical structure.

data base for the applications program and as the source structure for the display-scanning routine.

The disadvantage of the stored-data structure is that the applications program must use a structure of a particular form which may be unsuitable for the problem. The applications data may not have any particular structure at all. Even when the applications data is structured, it may be a different sort of structuring. For example, the structure of Fig. 3.8 does not model the electrical connectivity within the filter. Electrical connectivity is best represented by another structure which links components to points which are electrically identical. Conceivably the graphical structure could be extended to include connectivity relations, but, if many non-graphical attributes and relations are represented, the structure and manipulations of it will become complex. It is then necessary to employ a subsystem responsible solely for handling the graphical data structure.

Graphical Structures as Display Files

A further saving of storage space is achieved by dispensing with the display file and letting the display processor operate directly from the graphical data structure. The display processor must be sufficiently powerful to do this. It must have a subroutine facility, and it must be able to cope with any transformations it finds. There is no need for a scanning routine or for transformation routines, and the system reduces to that shown in Fig. 3.10. The system is compact, and the display is guaranteed to be an up-to-date representation of the data base. However, the graphical data structure loses much flexibility. The display processor is simple and fixed compared with a software scanning routine. The data structure must comply with these limitations, making the task of the applications program more difficult.

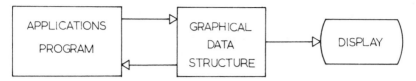

Figure 3.10. System with a graphical data structure acting as the display file.

Let us suppose a rotated copy is to be made of a symbol in the graphical data structure. The display processor cannot handle rotations, so the applications program must itself obtain the coordinates of the symbol, rotate them, and insert the result into the data structure. However, the coordinates are disguised as display commands, and must be converted to numbers before processing and back again to display commands after processing. Furthermore, the coordinates will be in the display processor's low-precision fixed-point format rather than the high-precision floating-point format preferred for operations such as rotation. Finally, the new symbol must be inserted into the graphical data structure with great care. This is because the display processor is displaying the structure while simultaneously the applications program is modifying it. Should the display processor encounter a subroutine pointer that (temporarily) indicates a non-display part of store, it will follow the pointer and try to obey what it finds and the picture will be lost. In order to avoid this, the applications program must stop the display processor while changing from old to new structures. The picture is lost during this period, but the period of loss can be reduced by employing some sort of double-buffering technique. Complex and arbitrary demands are made on the applications program because it has to handle the hardware of the display, in addition to its own applications task.

There is one situation in which it is acceptable to have the applications program and the display processor share the same data structure; this is where the application is itself concerned with two-dimensional geometry. There are only a small number of these applications. Most programs of this type concern themselves with building up and editing pictures, a process which may be done more easily with a pencil and paper. The programs are useful in situations where a picture has to be coded in some way, say for transmission to a graph plotter, to a remote computer, or to another program. The "applications" part of the program operates after the graphical structure has been built up, and consists of scanning the structure and translating it into object code.

Transformations

The four primitive transformations that are applied to an object in two dimensions are *shifting, scaling, rotation,* and *clipping*. The transformations apply to the coordinates of all points and end-points of lines forming the object.

In what follows, the coordinates of a point before transformation will be represented by (x, y), and after transformation by (x', y').

Shifting. An object is shifted relative to the origin by a distance D_x in the x direction, and a distance D_y in the y direction. The transformed point (x', y') is calculated by

$$x' = x + D_x$$
$$y' = y + D_y.$$

Scaling. An object is scaled (up or down) by multiplying its coordinates by a scaling factor S (greater or less than 1). The magnification or reduction is relative to the origin; a scaled-up object which is distant from the origin is moved further away as well as being magnified. Unequal scalings (S_x, S_y) may be applied to each axis, in which case the object is compressed or attenuated. If the factor scaling an axis is negative, then the object is reflected about that axis. The calculation is

$$x' = xS_x$$
$$y' = yS_y.$$

Rotation. The calculation

$$x' = x\cos\theta + y\sin\theta$$
$$y' = y\cos\theta - x\sin\theta$$

rotates the point (x, y) clockwise through θ rad around the origin, to give the transformed point (x', y').

A special case occurs when rotations are restricted to multiples of $\pi/2$. The new coordinates can then be found without the need for multiplication or for trigonometrical functions. For rotation by $n\pi/2$ the following relations hold:

$$
\begin{array}{lll}
n = 0 & x' = x & y' = y \\
n = 1 & x' = y & y' = -x \\
n = 2 & x' = -x & y' = -y \\
n = 3 & x' = -y & y' = x
\end{array}
$$

For $n \geqslant 4$, rotation by $n\pi/2$ is equivalent to rotation by $m\pi/2$ where m is the remainder of the integer division $n/4$.

Clipping. The clipping transformation applies a rectangular area to the set of points $[x, y]$ and produces from it a subset $[x', y']$ of points which lie within the area. The sides of the clipping rectangle are parallel with the coordinate axes. Let us suppose the rectangle is defined by specifying coordinates of opposite corners (Fig. 3.11); the coordinates of the lower corner are (x_L, y_L) and of the upper corner are (x_U, y_U). Then a point in $[x, y]$ is copied to $[x', y']$ only if all of the four conditions

$$x \geqslant x_L$$
$$x \leqslant x_U$$
$$y \geqslant y_L$$
$$y \leqslant y_U$$

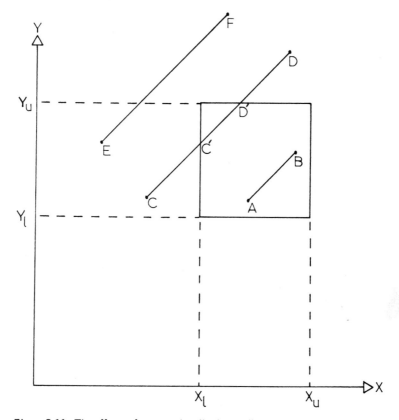

Figure 3.11. The effects of rectangular clipping on lines.

are true. This test applies to individual points. The case where points specify the ends of a line is more complicated. Figure 3.11 shows some conditions which can occur. Points A and B both lie within the clipping rectangle and so does the line defined by them. Points E and F, and their line, all lie outside the rectangle and can be rejected. However, points C and D lie outside the rectangle but part of the line joining them is visible within the rectangle. The new points C′ and D′ must be computed.

Let us suppose the line joining (a, b) and (c, d) is to be clipped by the rectangle with opposite corners (x_L, y_L) and (x_U, y_U). We can immediately reject any line lying completely to the left, to the right, above, or below the rectangle (lines AB, CD, EF, GH in Fig. 3.12). The condition is that any of the following be true:

$$x_L \geqslant \max(a, c)$$
$$x_U \leqslant \min(a, c)$$
$$y_L \geqslant \max(b, d)$$
$$y_U \leqslant \min(b, d).$$

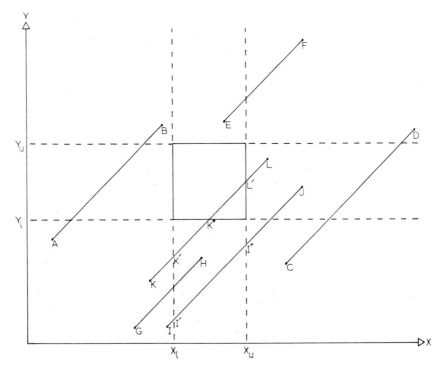

Figure 3.12. More details of rectangular clipping on straight lines.

If the line is not rejected by this test, we find whether it crosses a continued edge of the clipping rectangle:

if $x_L > \min(a, c)$　　the line crosses　$x = x_L$
if $x_U < \max(a, c)$　　the line crosses　$x = x_U$
if $y_L > \min(b, d)$　　the line crosses　$y = y_L$
if $y_U < \max(b, d)$　　the line crosses　$y = y_U$.

If none of these conditions is true, then the line lies totally within the clipping rectangle.

If the line does cross one of the continued edges, we calculate a new end-point at the intersection, discarding that part of the line lying away from the rectangle, as follows. If the line crosses $x = x_L$, we replace the point having the lesser x coordinate by the new point

$$[x_L, b + (x_L - a)(d - b)/(c - a)].$$

If the line crosses $x = x_U$, we replace the point having the greater x coordinate by the new point

$$[x_U, b + (x_U - a)(d - b)/(c - a)].$$

If the line crosses $y = y_L$, we replace the point having the lesser y coordinate by the new point

$$[a + (y_L - b)(c - a)/(d - b), y_L].$$

If the line crosses $y = y_U$, we replace the point having the greater y coordinate by the new point

$$[a + (y_U - b)(c - a)/(d - b), y_U].$$

After calculating the new end-point, we have a new line to which we reapply the whole process. For a line completely outside the clipping rectangle, in the *worst case*, two end-point calculations are made before the line is rejected. In Fig. 3.12, applying the tests in the order given above, line IJ is reduced to I′J, then to I″J, and then rejected. For the *worst case* of a line entering the clipping rectangle, three end-point calculations must be made. In Fig. 3.12, line KL is reduced to K′L, then to K′L′, then to K″L′, which is found to lie completely inside.

The Windowing Transformation

Windowing is a frequently used composite transformation made up from clipping, scaling, shifting, and sometimes rotation. The "window" is a rectangular area in the input space. Material within the window is projected onto the "viewport", a rectangular area in the output space. Usually the viewport is kept fixed while the window moves over the input space. The window is made larger to give an overall view of the input space in the viewport, and made smaller to "zoom" in on detail. Sometimes the window can be rotated in order to tilt the image seen through the viewport.

The windowing transformation is started by clipping off all material outside the window. It is important that this be the first stage, since it reduces the amount of material to be transformed in subsequent stages. The material remaining is then scaled to fit the viewport, and shifted to the viewport position.

If the window can be tilted, the clipping operation has to be done using a rectangle whose sides are not parallel with the coordinate axes. This is very time consuming. It may be more efficient to scale and shift first, and then to clip to the viewport rectangle. If the window is very small, it is best to clip twice, first to a rectangle big enough to contain the whole rectangle, however

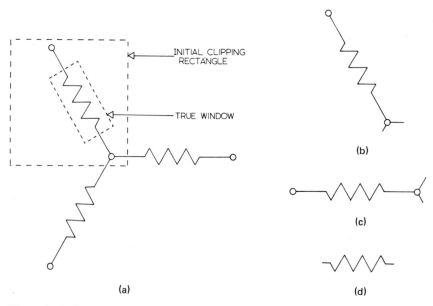

Figure 3.13. Primitive transformations making up the windowing transformation: (a) input space; (b) clip to initial rectangle; (c) rotate, scale, and shift to bring the window image within the viewport; (d) clip to the viewport.

tilted, but small enough to screen out significant amounts of material. After scaling and shifting, the second clipping is carried out using the viewport (Fig. 3.13).

Compilation of Transformations

A structured picture is built from subpictures, and usually each subpicture has one or more transformations operating upon it. A subpicture may itself be built up from other transformed subpictures. Figure 3.14a shows such a structure. The structure may be modeled by a data structure, or it may be represented by nested procedure calls. As the scanning routine interprets the data structure, or the procedure calls each other, the structure is traced through to the terminal data. Figure 3.14b shows the transformations in effect at each level. As the level increases, long strings of transformations can be built up.

Typically, the transformations are applied to hundreds of elements making up a picture, and can take up considerable time. If, as suggested in Fig. 3.14b,

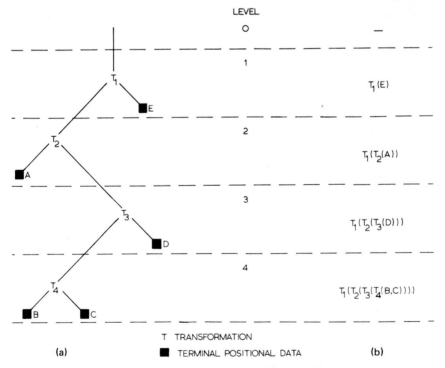

Figure 3.14. Structure of a compiled transformation: (a) total picture; (b) total transformation.

the transformations are applied one after the other, the time taken is multiplied by the number of transformations applied. Computation time can be shortened by reducing the string of primitive transformations into one overall transformation, which is then applied once only to the positional data.

When clipping is used, great reductions in computation time are possible if whole subpictures, which after being expanded would lie outside the clipping region, could be eliminated before being expanded. In order to do this the extent of the subpicture must be stored with the subpicture definition (i.e., when the subpicture is defined some sort of dimensioning statement must be included).

The Overall Transformation

Any sequence of primitive transformations, with one exception, can be combined into one overall transformation. The combining process takes the various clipping, scaling, shifting, and rotation operations, and produces a resultant clipping rectangle which will be denoted by (x_L, y_L, x_U, y_U) and resultant transformation parameters which will be denoted by a, b, c, d, e, f. The overall transformation is finally applied to the coordinates by first clipping $[x, y]$ to the rectangle (x_L, y_L, x_U, y_U), and then using a, b, c, d, e, f to operate on the remaining points to produce the transformed points $[x', y']$.

$$x' = ax + by + c$$
$$y' = dx + ey + f$$

Initially, the clipping rectangle is set to cover the whole display screen, and $a = e = 1, b = c = d = f = 0$. This defines an identity transformation.

At every *shift* by an x distance D_x and a y distance D_y

$$c := c + D_x$$
$$f := f + D_y$$

and the clipping rectangle is shifted in the opposite direction:

$$x_L := x_L - D_x$$
$$x_U := x_U - D_x$$
$$y_L := y_L - D_y$$
$$y_U := y_U - D_y.$$

At every *scaling* by S_x in the x direction, and S_y in the y direction

$$a := aS_x$$
$$b := bS_x$$
$$c := cS_x$$
$$d := dS_y$$
$$e := eS_y$$
$$f := fS_y$$

and the clipping rectangle is scaled inversely:

$$x_L := x_L/S_x$$
$$x_U := x_U/S_x$$
$$y_L := y_L/S_y$$
$$y_U := y_U/S_y$$

At every *clipping* the current clipping rectangle is compared with the new, and the area common to both becomes the new clipping area. If no area is common, the fact can be transmitted back to the scanning routine, which abandons all data controlled by the transformation. If a subpicture is accompanied by information specifying its dimensions, this can be used to reduce the current clipping area, since the dimensions indicate the extent of the subpicture, outside of which there is no data. If the expansion of a subpicture can be avoided because it lies completely outside the clipping area, a great deal of processing can be saved. Let us suppose that the new clipping rectangle (or subpicture dimensions) is specified by (x_L', y_L', x_U', y_U'). If $x_U < x_L'$ or $x_U' < x_L$ or $y_U < y_L'$ or $y_U' < y_L$, then there is no common clipping area and further data controlled by this transformation can be ignored. Otherwise,

$$x_L := \max(x_L, x_L')$$
$$y_L := \max(y_L, y_L')$$
$$x_U := \min(x_U, x_U')$$
$$y_U := \min(y_U, y_U').$$

At every *rotation* by θ radians,

$$a := a\cos\theta + d\sin\theta$$
$$b := b\cos\theta + e\sin\theta$$
$$c := c\cos\theta + f\sin\theta$$
$$d := d\cos\theta - a\sin\theta$$
$$e := e\cos\theta - b\sin\theta$$
$$f := f\cos\theta - c\sin\theta.$$

The combination of clipping followed by rotation is the one exception that cannot be reduced to a single overall transformation (unless the rotation is restricted to multiples of $\pi/2$). This is because clipping is carried out first to prevent unnecessary transformations on data that will later be discarded. Thus rotation tilts the clipping area with respect to the axes, violating the restriction that the rectangle edges must be parallel to the axes. Moreover, an attempt to combine another clipping rectangle with the tilted one will produce a shape that is not rectangular. In order to avoid these problems, the clipping must occur *after* the rotation and cannot be combined with subsequent clipping operations.

The computation-saving effects of applying clipping before other transformations can still be retained by performing a separate initial clipping operation using a rectangle that is large enough to contain a rotated version of the final rectangle. This gives an approximate initial clipping which is not accurate enough to select one part of a subpicture but will eliminate much irrelevant surrounding material. If the approximate clipping rectangle is not centered on the origin, then as well as being enlarged its center must be rotated by $-\theta$ radians to bring it back over the subpicture.

If the general rotation facility is omitted, allowing only rotations by multiples of $\pi/2$, the transformation system becomes simpler. In particular transformed clipping areas are always rectangular. A rotation of $4n\pi/2$ has no effect. The effects of the other possible rotations are shown in Table 3.1.

Display Files

Data emerges from the transformational routines in the form of point and line coordinates. A final process converts them to instructions capable of driving the display processor, and places them into the display file. In its simplest form, the display file contains a string of these instructions, ending with a

Table 3.1. Transformation Effects for Rotations of $n\pi/2$.[1]

Rotation	$(4n + 1)\pi/2$	$(4n + 2)\pi/2$	$(4n + 3)\pi/2$
Effects	$a := d$	$a := -a$	$a := -d$
	$b := e$	$b := -b$	$b := -e$
	$c := f$	$c := -c$	$c := -f$
	$d := -a$	$d := -d$	$d := a$
	$e := -b$	$e := -e$	$e := b$
	$f := -c$	$f := -f$	$f := c$
	$x_L := -y_U$	$x_L := -x_U$	$x_L := y_L$
	$x_U := -y_L$	$x_U := -x_L$	$x_U := y_U$
	$y_L := x_L$	$y_L := -y_U$	$y_L := -x_U$
	$y_U := x_U$	$y_U := -y_L$	$y_U := -x_L$

[1] n is an integer.

jump instruction back to the start of the file. However, most display files can be *structured* using jumps and subroutine calls.

Figure 3.15 shows a display file structured into fixed blocks that will be called *frames*. A frame corresponds to a graphical substructure, or to a frame procedure. The display code produced from the substructure or frame procedure enters only the block reserved for it. The concluding instruction is a subroutine return. A frame can be altered in isolation without having to recompile the whole display structure, and whole frames can be added to and removed from the display by altering single instructions in the main display cycle. This improves response times. However, some sort of store management of the display file is required. If too much material is added to a frame, the display code will overflow its allotted block. The store-management program must then allocate another block for the overflow and connect it by a jump instruction. A table defines unused blocks and those which belong to specific frames. If a frame recompiles into a smaller space than before and uses fewer blocks, then the unused blocks are returned to the common pool.

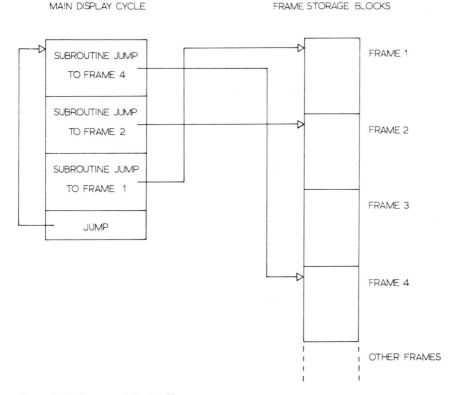

Figure 3.15. Structured display file.

Graphical Input

A graphical input device selects a point in 2-space, usually in the same coordinate system as the display. By itself, the information is not of much use unless the applications program is concerned only with pictures, drawn in terms of the display. In order to be of use, the input point must be related to the categories with which the applications program deals, for example, resistors, filters, and circuits.

One way of identifying the structure which corresponds to the input point is to go through the whole process of generating the picture, and arresting the process when a generated point matches the input point. The record is then available of all the subpictures and operations invoked in the generation of the point. The point may be at the end of a line in the third resistor of the second filter of the circuit under consideration. The point is identified in terms of the categories line, resistor, filter, and circuit, and as such can be transmitted to the applications program which will have selected the level of categories it wants.

The regeneration of a whole picture takes a considerable amount of time. The delay can be reduced by specifying a small initial clipping rectangle around the input point. Subpictures lying outside the clipping region will not be evaluated and the process will be speeded. The data produced in this case should not be sent to the display file since the picture, apart from the clipping region around the input point, would vanish. However, let us suppose that the data base has changed since the picture was last completely output. The change will not be apparent at the time the input identification is made, because the new data is not being sent to the display file. In this case it is better to identify the input by generating the picture in full and allowing the generated data to go to the display file.

An alternative method uses the display file to identify the indicated object. The display processor is interrupted when the point it generates matches the input point, thus identifying the responsible display file element. Enough information is associated with the responsible element to identify the indicated object. Whenever a point is linked by a one-to-one relation with the object that produced it, identification can be made by computing the inverse relation. Programs which plot algebraic functions on the display can fall into this class. An extreme case occurs where the same data structure is used for data base and for display file. Where a many-to-one mapping is possible, there is no alternative to testing the many source objects to see which ones generate the point, although knowledge of the responsible display file instruction can cut down the search. For example, if the display file is organized as suggested in Fig. 3.15, then an input point can be located within a frame, and only objects in that frame need be considered.

Handling Graphical Input Devices

The two basic tasks of an input device are to indicate objects on the display, and to input two-coordinate data not necessarily corresponding to anything being displayed.

The light pen performs the first task. Positioned over the indicated object, it generates an interrupt whenever the display processor deals with the object. However, it can be used only to signal points which lie on displayed objects. In order to indicate an arbitrary point, the program must be persuaded to display something there. One approach is to cover the whole display with a raster of points. More common, however, is the use of a tracking symbol (usually a cross). If the light pen is placed at the periphery of the symbol, the program repositions the symbol so that its center lies under the light pen. The tracking symbol will follow movements of the light pen. Some programs [e.g. (1)] move the tracking symbol to an anticipated position based on the current velocity of the light-pen movement.

Devices such as tablets and tracker balls can generate and input two-coordinate data independently from the display. The program must display a cursor symbol (such as a cross) centered on the point currently generated by the tablet so that the operator has visual feedback of the input. However, the tablet or tracker ball cannot by itself identify the display-file instruction currently generating the object at the cursor position. A comparator (2, 3) can be used if available. This accepts coordinates such as the cursor position, and generates an interrupt when a point is displayed at those coordinates. In the absence of a comparator, the display file must be searched for points at the cursor position and for lines which cross the cursor position.

A device such as a tablet gives a continuous positional input, and means must exist to indicate whether the input is significant. A button may be provided which interrupts the processor when pressed and causes it to read the position. Alternatively, the button may cause a series of interrupts until it is released. In cases where a device produces a series of interrupts, the computer should accept, at each interrupt, only inputs that have significantly different coordinate values from those at the last interrupt.

Light-pen tracking is usually done by an independent service routine and does not generate interrupts. Attention must be drawn to the light pen by some other device such as a keyboard. Alternatively, an attention region can be described around the original position of the tracking symbol when tracking starts. The service routine generates an interrupt if the tracking symbol crosses the boundary of the region.

Visual Feedback of Inputs

The result of each input operation must be repeated on the display, so that the operator can appreciate the effect of his input and take corrective action if necessary. The more immediate and complete this feedback, the easier the operator's task, but, unfortunately, the greater the load on the computer.

At the lowest level, the operator inputs a point which can be fed back on the display as a cursor position. At least this amount of feedback is essential. At a higher level the operator may want to input a line. He sets the cursor position at one end of the line and then signals (by a switch, button, or keyboard) that he wishes to draw a line. He moves the cursor to the other end of the line and signals that the line is complete. The program then draws the line between the two points. Although this is satisfactory, visual feedback is improved if the line is continually redrawn between the initial point and the cursor position. Similarly, a subpicture such as a resistor may be positioned by setting the cursor to the required position and signaling that a resistor should be generated. Visual feedback is improved if the resistor symbol actually accompanies the cursor as it moves about the screen.

Positioning operations may be aided by the provision of a scaled grid or a matrix of points against which the operator can gauge the position of his input. Alternatively, the current numerical values of the cursor coordinates can be displayed.

In positioning operations, visual feedback is given by causing an indicated object to stand out in some way, such as making it brighter or causing it to flash regularly. If pointing is combined with positioning, i.e., an object is "picked up" by the cursor and then moved around, the fact that the object follows the cursor provides sufficient feedback to distinguish the object. Pointing can be made easier by allowing the cursor to pick up all objects within a small region about it. In a combined pointing and positioning operation, the cursor appears to have a magnetic field and attracts to itself all objects within the pick-up region.

Graphical Input of Non-Graphical Information

An operator at a display console will sometimes have to input keyboard data to the applications program, and it may be inconvenient for him to alternate his attention between keyboard and display. This leads to the use of the graphics to input what is essentially keyboard data. The most common method is to display a *menu* of small symbols called *light buttons*, each of which is connected with some input function. The presence of the input cursor inside a light button invokes the corresponding function. The menu can be rapidly changed to give different lists of available functions. The technqiue can be extended to simulate a complete keyboard by light buttons.

Numerical data is sometimes input using a linear *potentiometer*. One end of the potentiometer represents high numbers, the other end low numbers. The actual number is displayed over the potentiometer, and changes as the input cursor moves from one end of the potentiometer to the other. Variations of this technique exist where the potentiometer has a non-linear scale, or controls the rate of change of the input number. The *light handle* (4) is a side-by-side array of potentiometers of varying sensitivities, allowing coarser or finer adjustments of the number.

3.3. RELATED SOFTWARE AIDS AND TECHNIQUES

Data Structures for Interactive Graphics

In general, a graphical system contains three groupings of data: the data base for the applications program, the data structure representing the display, and the display file. Many systems combine the applications data base with the display structure, or the display structure with the display file.

The applications program data base should be designed to suit the application. There is no need to make it flexible or highly structured if the application doe not demand it. For example, a scientific program may calculate values of a function for plotting. The program's data base will contain values and ranges for the function arguments and not much else, and will remain fixed in extent throughout the operation of the program.

The data structures representing the display, including the display file, will usually change in size unpredictably during the run of an interactive program. The function-plotting program may produce plots with varying numbers of points. In structured displays parts of the structure may expand and contract while other parts remain unchanged. The display data structure and the display file must therefore be dynamic and flexible. Additionally, structures which serve both the display and the applications program must possess general data-handling facilities. These can be summarized as the ability to define new associations between various parts of the data, to trace and locate related items of data, and to add and remove data elements (5). An example of a structured picture is shown in Fig. 3.16. As the circuit is built up, the structure will alter. Additions and deletions may occur at any point. If a picture element is discarded, the subpictures it contains may also be discarded, provided that they are not part of some other picture element. Thus if both filters in Fig. 3.16 were to be discarded, the circle, the capacitor, and the dashed box could also be discarded, but not the resistor.

The structure shown in Fig. 3.16 contains more than just graphical data; it also contains names and values for the components. The structure could be used to build up a circuit diagram, and to assign names and values to the components. However, the structure is inadequate to provide a data base for a circuit-analysis program. Circuit analysis is concerned not with lines and positions, but with electrical components and their interconnection. The structure of Fig. 3.16 must be processed to yield the more useful structure

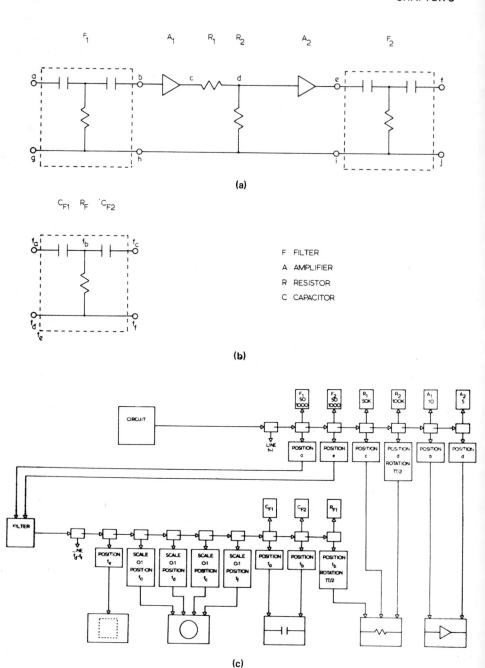

Figure 3.16. A structured picture: (a) circuit picture; (b) filter sub-picture; (c) graphical structure.

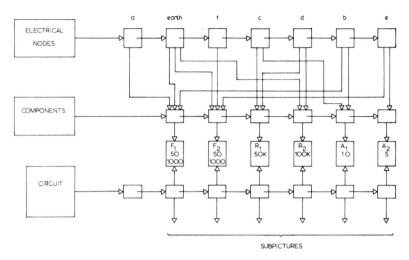

Figure 3.17. Applications-oriented structure.

of Fig. 3.17. Two new data types are created, electrical components and inter-connection nodes, and are associated with the original display structure. Further classification can be done similarly; i.e., a data type could be created which linked together all the resistors in the circuit, or all the amplifiers.

Mapping the Data Structure
onto the Computer Store

The hardware organization of a computer store is linear and fixed; items are ordered sequentially. The various structures described above have arbitrary orderings and are dynamic. Software maps the abstract onto the concrete.

The *linked list* (6) shown in Fig. 3.18 can handle dynamically changing lists of items. At any point in the list an item can be added, deleted, or replaced by a list of items (Figs. 3.19 and 3.20) without disturbing the rest of the structure. Each element of the list is composed of an ordered pair of addresses. A marker associated with each address indicates whether the address is of another list element or of a piece of data. One specific address (usually zero) is reserved to indicate termination of the list. New relationships can be established among the data by creating new ordered address pairs (Fig. 3.21).

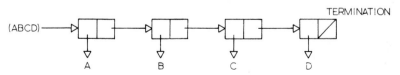

Figure 3.18. The linked list of items (ABCD).

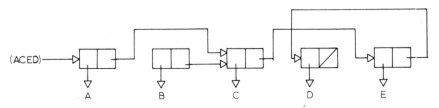

Figure 3.19. List (ABCD) changed to (ACED).

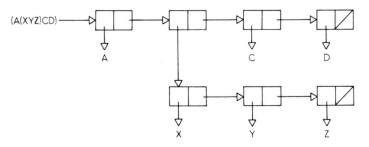

Figure 3.20. List (ABCD) after B has been changed to the linked list of items (XYZ).

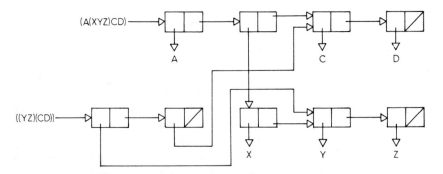

Figure 3.21. Creating the new association [(YZ) (CD)].

Before a list structure is created, the available store is collected into the *free list*, which is a list of unused elements. If a new element is required to build a list structure, it is taken from the free list. If an element is deleted from a list structure, it can either be returned to the free list or left "floating", as is the second element shown in Fig. 3.19. Floating elements are periodically returned to the free list by a routine called the *garbage collector*.

If a particular sequence of items is always fixed, there is no need to link the items with address pointers since the items can be stored sequentially in a block. The ordered pair is generalized to an ordered multiple of any number of items; the items can be data or addresses of other multiples. A structure built with

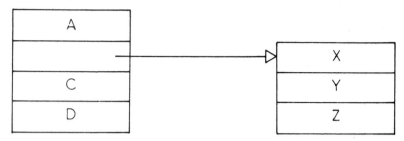

Figure 3.22. The list [A(XYZ)CD] in plex form.

these blocks is called a *plex structure* (7). Figure 3.22 shows the list structure of Fig. 3.20 in plex form. Means must exist to determine the length of each block either by marking the last element, or by keeping a length integer in the block, or by restricting all the blocks to the same length. Garbage collection is complicated by having to deal with blocks of varying sizes. Sometimes garbage collection compacts the data in use to one end of the store so that all free storage lies in one continuous block.

A linked list in which the last element points back to the start of the list is known as a *ring*. Any item in a ring is accessible from any other item. Often one element is singled out as the start of the ring.

Additional pointers can be included in a list element. Back pointers allow the ring to be traced in either direction. Each element in a ring structure may have a pointer back to the ring start. This speeds up accesses to the structure but tends to be wasteful of storage. As a consequence store-saving schemes have been devised (8) such as storing back and start pointers in alternate elements (Fig. 3.23).

The structures described above all satisfy the requirement of storing dynamic data, and allowing it to be added and removed at any point. There remains the requirement of establishing new associations between the various data elements.

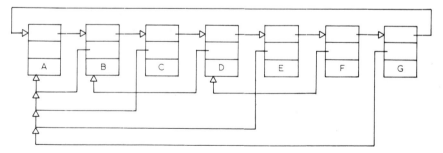

Figure 3.23. Ring structure with back and start pointers in alternate elements.

If the number of associations from a specific data element is constant, a plex element may be used to hold both data and pointers to associated data elements. The number of associations cannot be increased without also enlarging the plex element, so in cases where unpredictable numbers of new associations arise only one association pointer is stored with the data. The association pointer indicates a dynamic list (or ring) of elements, each of which contains a pointer to the associated data. In a complex situation with many relationships, the structure may become composed of long richly interconnected chains, making garbage collection and access to data slow.

An alternative method of defining associations between data elements is to store the associations in a separate table. The relationship between items is found by a table look-up. Hash-coding techniques can be used to make the table access fast and efficient (9, 10).

Programming Languages for Interactive Computer Graphics

The language in which the applications program is written must be able both to program the application and to handle graphic devices. The first requirement demands that the language has good general-purpose facilities, so suitable languages tend to be general-purpose high-level programming languages extended to handle graphics. The appearance and ease of use of the extensions depends on how they are implemented. Readable and easily understood formats usually involve changes to the syntax and compiler of the language. Simpler implementations use subroutine or procedure calls defined within the existing language syntax, and cannot fail to be more opaque and obscure.

An interactive graphics program involves a dialog between program and operator. The programmer has to define the limits of the dialog; he has to invent a command language and provide a program to handle its syntax. This task can be programmed in a general-purpose high-level language, but is easier in interactive languages such as POP-2 (11) which have their own syntax-analysis abilities available as a programmable function. Alternatively, the general language can be extended to have dialog-handling facilities (12, 13, 14).

Desirable features of a programming language are clarity and conciseness. If we want to define a triangle by the line segments lying between (0, 0), (10, 10), and (0, 10), and call it TRIANGLE, then a reasonably direct way is as follows.

```
DEFINE TRIANGLE
LINE FROM (0, 0) TO (10, 10) TO (0, 10) TO (0, 0)
END TRIANGLE
```

If we then want to display the triangle rotated through an angle θ and placed at (20, 20) then a reasonably direct way to program it is as follows.

TRIANGLE ROTATED (θ) AT (20, 20)

A system similar to this has been described by Newman (15). Such a system would need changes to the language compiler to handle the syntax, and it would require run-time routines to handle the transformations. These language changes can be avoided, at the expense of clarity, by denoting a graphical function by a procedure call of the host language.

CALL DEFINE ("TRIANGLE")
CALL LINE (0, 0, 10, 10)
CALL LINE (10, 10, 0, 10)
CALL LINE (0, 10, 0, 0)
CALL ENDEFINE

The triangle rotated by θ and moved to (20, 20) would be denoted as follows.

CALL DEFINE ("ROTATEDTRIANGLE")
CALL ROTATE (θ)
CALL SETXY (20, 20)
CALL DRAW ("TRIANGLE")
CALL ENDEFINE

The subroutine calls build up a data structure which is interpreted by a scanning routine to produce the display file.

At a lower level of display system, the programmer must organize the construction of the display file himself. He could probably construct the TRIANGLE file by the same sort of program as shown above, but he must himself deal with the transformation calculations. Host languages with special provision for array and matrix operations lead to compact programming of transformations.

Input Facilities

Data from input devices usually needs processing into a useful form before being sent to the applications program, and this is best done by system routines which are invisible to the programmer. An example is light-pen tracking; the system routine responsible for moving the tracking symbol should be invisible to the programmer, who simply asks for the current tracking position. Other useful system functions are the provision of an interrupt whenever the cursor (or tracking symbol) enters or leaves a specified area of the screen (this can be used for light buttons), and transmission of information about part of a picture picked out by a light pen or comparator.

Information is transferred from the system routines to the applications program through reserved variable names. If the names PENX, PENY are reserved to mean the current x, y positions of the cursor or tracking cross, then the applications program can obtain the values by statements like the following.

A := PENX

Names can be reserved in a similar way for light buttons.

IF LBUT1 THEN . . .

Interrupts can be transmitted by making them set a logical (Boolean) reserved variable. Such a variable may be reset explicitly by the program, or automatically each time the program accesses the variable.

Alterations to the language compiler will be necessary if the reserved names are to be treated specially. For this reason, reserved variables are often implemented as zero-argument functions which return the input data as their output values.

A light-pen "hit" produces an unpredictable amount of information. The whole hierarchy of structures which produced the point seen by the light pen is available for transmission to the applications program. The complete record needs to be contained in a flexible data structure, such as a stack. Alternatively, the applications program may specify which items are to be reported in a light-pen hit. If any item is a subpicture in another item, the higher-level item is selected; thus only one datum need be transferred. This facility enables the display to be selectively responsive to light-pen detects; i.e., the light pen can be set to pick up points but not lines, lines but not points, electronic components, subcircuits, and so on. Items can be made responsive by a statement of the form

ENABLE LINE, CAPACITOR, FILTER

and made unresponsive by a corresponding DISABLE statement. The items indicated by the light pen can be reported to the applications program in the form of a pointer or reference to the appropriate part of the graphics data structure (or display program). Some systems allow labels to be assigned to parts of the display, in which case the nearest label is reported (16).

Implementations

Host languages that have been extended for graphics include FORTRAN (17), ALGOL-60 (7, 10), PL/1 (16), and APL (18). Other important systems are described in references (12) and (15).

Software Function Generation

Three Dimensions. A solid such as a cube may be conveniently represented by the coordinates of its vertices and the line segments that form the edges between the vertices. Transformations in three dimensions are analogous to their two-dimensional counterparts. A point (x, y, z) may be transformed into (x', y', z') by shifting, scaling, and rotation about an axis. In order to shift (x, y, z) through D_x in the x direction, D_y in the y direction, and D_z in the z direction

$$x' := x + D_x$$
$$y' := y + D_y$$
$$z' := z + D_z.$$

A solid may be magnified or reduced by a factor S_x in the x direction, S_y in the y direction, and S_z in the z direction by

$$x' := xS_x$$
$$y' := yS_y$$
$$z' := zS_z.$$

In a right-handed coordinate system, a point may be rotated clockwise by θ radians around the x axis by

$$x' := x$$
$$y' := y\cos\theta + z\sin\theta$$
$$z' := z\cos\theta - y\sin\theta.$$

Rotation about the y axis is carried out by

$$x' := x\cos\theta - z\sin\theta$$
$$y' := y$$
$$z' := z\cos\theta + x\sin\theta.$$

Rotation about the z axis is carried out by

$$x' := x\cos\theta + y\sin\theta$$
$$y' := y\cos\theta - x\sin\theta$$
$$z' := z.$$

A pictorial representation of the solid may be obtained by a perspective projection onto a plane. Let us suppose that an observer is looking towards the point (x, y, z) in a positive direction along the z axis from a viewpoint situated at a distance $(-p)$ from the origin (Fig. 3.24). The perspective projection (x', y') of the point onto the xy plane at $z = 0$ is

$$x' = px/(p + z)$$
$$y' = py/(p + z).$$

A straight-line segment can be handled by projecting the end-points onto the plane and then generating a new straight line between them.

A straightforward projection of a solid onto the viewing plane transforms all the edges and vertices, including those which would normally be hidden from view. A more realistic projection can be made if the hidden elements are removed. For any reasonably complex three-dimensional scene, this involves a great deal of computation. The time delay makes hidden-line elimination

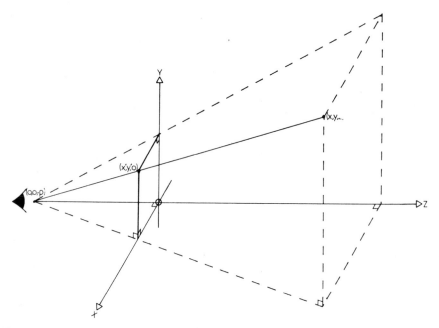

Figure 3.24. Perspective projection.

unsuitable for an interactive environment. The problem of minimizing the amount of computation is difficult and has attracted much attention (19-23). The development of displays which can render shading of surfaces has led to the development of algorithms for hidden-surface removal and for shading (24-28).

Generating Straight and Curved Lines by Software. The pictures generated by a graphics program are composed of points and (ideally) continuous lines, both straight and curved. The common VDU is capable of generating only discrete points on a fixed grid, and this creates the problem of how best to choose points to represent a continuous line. There may be a noticeable gap between the proper line position and the nearest grid point, and in these cases the grid points must be chosen to give a good approximation to the line (Fig. 3.25). Most displays have the facility to generate vectors between specified points and a few can generate circles and other functions, but for others the problem has to be handled by software. A similar problem occurs with digital plotters, which have to represent a continuous line by a series of short line segments which can lie in eight possible directions.

The important factors affecting the display of continuous lines are the size of the smallest increment on the display, the speed at which the display points can be calculated, the number of points which can be displayed, and the airthmetic facilities available. In the best possible situation, the smallest increment of the display is comparable to the spot size, and a large number of spots can be displayed side by side to create the impression of continuity; there are no restrictions on the computation time and the arithmetic facilities impose no restriction on the method used to calculate each point. Unfortunately, in a low-cost system all these features may be absent.

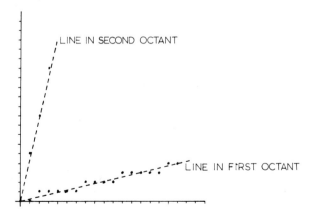

Figure 3.25. Straight-line approximations.

Straight Lines. A straightforward way of using n points to represent the straight line between (x_1, y_1) and (x_2, y_2) is to calculate each point (x_i, y_i) by

$$x_i = x_1 + \frac{i(x_2 - x_1)}{n - 1}$$

$$y_i = y_1 + \frac{i(y_2 - y_1)}{n - 1}$$

where $i = 0, 1, \ldots, (n-1)$. The value of n depends on the length of the line and the density of points on the line:

$n =$ (length of line) $\times$ (linear density of points)
$ = [(x_1 - x_2)^2 + (y_1 - y_2)^2]^{1/2} \times$ (linear density of points).

Such calculations are time consuming. The extraction of square roots is always a relatively lengthy process and can be avoided by estimating the length as $|x_1 - x_2| + |y_1 - y_2|$. Some machines do not have hardware for multiplication or division, and instead have to use lengthy subroutines. Each point of the line requires one division and two multiplications, so the generation of a line can take an unacceptable amount of time. A method is required that does not need multiplications or divisions at each point. If it is possible to calculate the quantities $q_x = (x_2 - x_1)/(n - 1)$ and $q_y = (y_2 - y_1)/(n - 1)$ before drawing the line, then each point can be found from the preceding point by two additions only:

$$x_i = x_{i-1} + q_x$$
$$y_i = y_{i-1} + q_y.$$

Unfortunately, in fixed-point arithmetic the quantities q_x and q_y may underflow the capacity of the computer word. A satisfactory line can be produced without multiplication or division by a software implementation of the *digital differential analyser.*

The Digital Differential Analyser. The digital differential analyser *(DDA)* can be used to generate curves as well as straight lines. The DDA is a digital version of the integrator of an analog computer, and, simulated on a digital computer, it can be used in much the same way as the analog machine to produce a digital approximation to the solution of a differential equation. This encompasses a vast variety of curves.

The basic component is an input accumulator of capacity k, into which samples of the input function can be added (see Fig. 3.26). The symbol a will

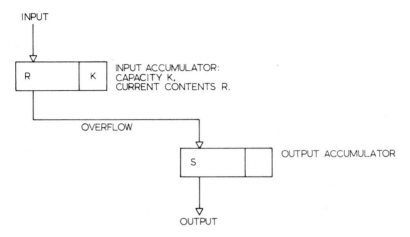

Figure 3.26. Basic components of a digital differential analyser.

denote the contents of the accumulator. When the accumulator receives an input that would cause a to exceed the capacity k (say $a = k + r$), the accumulator overflows into an output accumulator whose contents will be denoted by s. After overflow, the input accumulator retains the remainder value r. The total sum represented by the two accumulators is $ks + r$. The arrangement is shown in Fig. 3.26. If the accumulators are preset in the way shown below, and if the input accumulator receives samples of the input function $f(1), f(2), \ldots, f(x)$, then the value s held by the output accumulator will approximate to $\int_0^x f(i)\mathrm{d}i$. This is because the exact integral

$$F(x) = \int_0^x f(i)\mathrm{d}i$$

is defined by the limit

$$F(x) = \lim_{q \to \infty} \left[\frac{1}{q} \sum_{i=1}^{xq} f(i) + F(0) \right].$$

We compare this limit with the value s from the output accumulator. Let us suppose the initial values of r and s are r_0 and s_0 and that the input accumulator receives a sequence of inputs $f(1), f(2), \ldots, f(n)$. Then

$$sk + r = s_0 k + r_0 + \sum_{i=1}^{n} f(i)$$

from which

$$s = \frac{1}{k} \sum_{i=1}^{n} f(i) + \frac{r_0 - r}{k} + s_0.$$

Thus if we make the capacity k of the input accumulator equal to q and the initial value s_0 of the output accumulator equal to $F(0)$, then the value s approximates to the form of the limit which defined the integral $\int_0^x f(i) di$:

$$s = \left[\frac{1}{q} \sum_{i=1}^{n} f(i) + F(0) \right] + \frac{r_0 - r}{q}.$$

The value of s will not exactly equal the integral for two reasons: (i) q cannot be made infinite, but only very large; (ii) there is an error term $(r_0 - r)/q$ between s and the expression for the limit, arising because s is restricted to integer values. The best that can be done with the error term is to make it lie symmetrically about zero by setting the initial value r_0 to $q/2$; the error then lies between $-\frac{1}{2}$ and $+\frac{1}{2}$. The best that can be done with q is to make it as large as possible, but not so large that an appreciable amount of time is used up by repeated additions into the input accumulator.

Straight Lines by DDA. The straight line joining (x_1, y_1) and (x_2, y_2) can be represented by

$$x = x_1 + t$$
$$y = y_1 + \frac{t(y_2 - y_1)}{x_2 - x_1} \qquad 0 \leqslant t \leqslant x_2 - x_1.$$

We can generate the line by letting t move in steps of 1 from 0 to $x_2 - x_1$. The x coordinate is produced by a counter with initial contents x_1 incremented for every step in the value of t. The y coordinate can be produced by an integration:

$$y = y_1 + \int_0^t \frac{y_2 - y_1}{x_2 - x_1} dp \simeq y_1 + \frac{1}{x_2 - x_1} \sum_{i=0}^{t} (y_2 - y_1)$$

and we can approximate the integration with a DDA of capacity $x_2 - x_1$, constant input $y_2 - y_1$, and initial values of $(x_2 - x_1)/2$ for the input accumulator and y_1 for the output accumulator. A line produced by this method is shown in Fig. 3.25. The y coordinate value is approximate because y is restricted to integer values. However setting the initial contents of the input accumulator to half its capacity ensures that the error lies symmetrically about the true y value within $\pm\frac{1}{2}$, giving a balanced appearance to the line.

The line generator increases x in steps of unit length. This is satisfactory in the first octant but gives too few points in the second octant (see Fig. 3.25), where it is better to step the y value and use the DDA to calculate the corresponding x value. In the other octants one or both of the steps must be by negative amounts, and this must be taken into account by the line generator. An algorithm for generating a straight line between (x_1, y_1) and (x_2, y_2) in the first octant is given below.

The variables x, y, r are initialized thus:

$x := x_1$	x is the x position of a point.
$r := (x_2 - x_1)/2$	r is the input accumulator of the DDA.
$y := y_1$	y is the y position of a point and is given by the value in the output accumulator of the DDA.

The following procedure is executed $x_2 - x_1$ times to generate $x_2 - x_1$ points:

$x := x + 1$	Increment the x coordinate.
$r := r + (y_2 - y_1)$	Add the constant input $y_2 - y_1$ into the input accumulator of the DDA.
If $r \geqslant x_2 - x_1$ then	Test for overflow in the input accum-
$[r := r - (x_2 - x_1); y := y + 1]$	ulator; if there is overflow, increment the output accumulator leaving the remainder in the input accumulator.
Plot (x, y)	Generate a point on the display.

The DDA method of drawing straight lines is fast, since at most five additions are needed to compute the position of each point.

Generating Other Shapes by DDA. The DDA can be used to generate any curve which can be represented by a differential equation, in a manner similar to an analog computer. For example, a circle of radius a, centered at the origin, is described by

$$x = a\cos\theta$$
$$y = a\sin\theta.$$

Since

$$\sin \theta = \int_0^\theta \cos t \, dt$$

and

$$\cos \theta = -\int_0^\theta \sin t \, dt$$

we can generate values of $\sin \theta$ and $\cos \theta$ by the arrangement shown in Fig. 3.27. The analogous DDA arrangement, generating an approximation to the circle, is shown in Fig. 3.28. Two DDA units with capacity k are used. The initial values of the input accumulators are both set up to be $k/2$. The output accumulators are initially set to contain zero and a, the radius of the circle. The number of points plotted and the closeness of fit to the true circle depend on k, which determines how many slices were taken in computing the approximations to the integrals. The larger the value of k, the better the approximation.

Representing Simple Curves with a Fixed Number of Points. Some systems have a restriction on the number of points that can be displayed. For example, a curve may be calculated point by point and the coordinates stored in a buffer for display. There may be limitations on the size of the buffer or on the number of points that can be displayed without flicker. When the number of points representing the line is restricted it becomes important to space the points more closely where the line is tightly curved. A simple geometric curve such as an ellipse or parabola can often be represented in

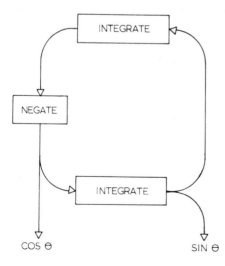

COS ϴ   SIN ϴ   **Figure 3.27.** Scheme for generating sin θ and cos θ.

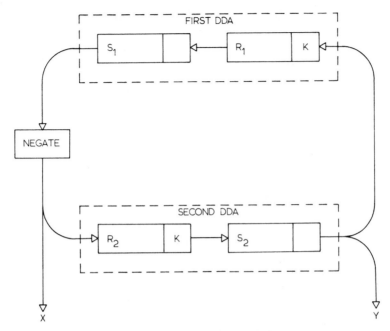

Figure 3.28. Arrangement of two DDA's to draw a circle.

terms of a single parameter. If the parameter is divided into equal increments, the points it produces are frequently closer together where the curvature is greater. An example is the ellipse.

The parametric equations for an ellipse with center (x_c, y_c) and with major and minor semi-axes a and b are

$$x = x_c + a\cos\theta\cos t - b\sin\theta\sin t$$
$$y = y_c + a\cos\theta\sin t - b\sin\theta\cos t$$

where t is the angle between the major axis and the x axis, and θ is the parameter. To plot n points, x and y are calculated for equal increments of $\theta = 2\pi i/(n-1)$ $(i = 0, 1, \ldots, n-1)$. With this representation the point spacing is inversely proportional to the curvature, and the ellipse will be represented adequately.

The time spent in the repeated calculation of the sine and cosine functions can be avoided by using trigonometrical identities. Sine and cosine functions are used only initially to find

$$p = \cos t$$
$$q = \sin t$$
$$r = \cos\left[2\pi/(n-1)\right]$$
$$s = \sin\left[2\pi/(n-1)\right].$$

Initially, $\theta = 0$ so $\cos \theta = 1$ and $\sin \theta = 0$. Subsequently, $\cos \theta$ and $\sin \theta$ can be found from their previous values:

$$\cos \theta_{i+1} = r\cos \theta_i - s\sin \theta_i$$
$$\sin \theta_{i+1} = s\cos \theta_i + r\sin \theta_i.$$

Algorithms for plotting other simple curves can be found in references (29) and (30).

3.4. CONCLUSION

This chapter has indicated many of the software techniques which have to be used in interactive computer graphics systems. It has shown that the choice of software elements is dictated by the needs of the application in the same way that input–output peripherals must be chosen to suit the needs of the operator. The way in which a system is designed so as to have desirable characteristics for its operators in its application is the subject of the final chapter.

We can make few hard and fast rules governing the choice of software for given tasks. The field of choice of techniques and software aids is too large. The most effective aid to the programmer is a knowledge of as many of the tools available as possible and good judgment as to the effectiveness of each in various situations. It is to be hoped that this chapter can point the interested programmer in the direction of useful information concerning the development of software tools for interactive computer graphics.

REFERENCES

1. Sutherland, I. E. SKETCHPAD: a man–machine graphical communication system. *Proc. SJCC 1963,* p. 329. Spartan Books, Baltimore, Md.
2. Farmer, N. A. A digital comparator for use with computer displays. *IEEE Trans. Comp.* **C18**, 269, 1969.
3. Konkle, K. H. An analog comparator as a pseudo light pen for computer displays. *IEEE Trans. Comp.* **C17**(1), 54, 1968.
4. Newman, W. M. A graphical technique for numerical input. *Comp. J.* **11**, 63, May 1968.
5. Knuth, D. E. *The Art of Computer Programming,* Vol. 1, Chap. 2. Addison Wesley, Reading, Mass.
6. *LISP 1.5 Programmer's Manual.* MIT Press, Cambridge, Mass.
7. Ross, D. T. *The AED Approach to Generalised Computer Aided Design.* Electronic Systems Lab., MIT, Rep. No. ESL-R 305, 1967.
8. Sutherland, W. R. *The CORAL Language and Data Structure.* Lincoln Lab., MIT, Rep. No. TR 405, 1966.

9. Crick, M. F., and Symonds, A. J. *A Software Associative Memory for Complex Data Structures.* IBM Cambridge Scientific Center Rep. No. g320-2060.
10. Rovner, P. D., and Feldman, J. A. The LEAP language and data structure. *Proc. IFIP Congress,* North-Holland, Amsterdam, 1968.
11. Burstall, R. M., Collins, J. S., and Popplestone, R. J. Programming in POP-2. Edinburgh University Press, Edinburgh, 1971.
12. Kulsrud, H. E. A general purpose graphic language. *Comm. ACM* **11**, 247, April 1968.
13. Newman, W. M. A system for interactive graphical programming. *Proc. SJCC 1968,* pp. 47–54, Thompson Book Co., Washington, D.C.
14. Stack, T. R., and Walker, S. T. AIDS: advanced interactive display system. *Proc. SJCC 1971,* pp. 113–121, AFIPS Press, Montrale, N.J.
15. Newman, W. M. Display procedures. *Comm. ACM,* **14**(10), 651, Oct. 1971.
16. Soop, K. The design and use of a PL/1 based graphic programming language. *Proc. Online 1972,* Vol. 2, p. 601. Brunel University, Uxbridge, UK, 1972.
17. Hurwitz, A., Citron, J. P., and Yeaton, J. B. GRAF: graphical extensions to FORTRAN. *Proc. SJCC 1967,* pp. 553–557, Thompson Book Co., Washington, D.C.
18. Giloi, W. K., Encarnacao, J., and Kestner, W. APL-G: APL extended for graphics. *Proc. Online 1972,* Vol. 2, p. 579. Brunel University, Uxbridge, UK, 1972.
19. Encarnacao, J. L. A survey of old and new solutions for the hidden line problem. *Symposium on Interactive Computer Grahpics, Delft, 1970.*
20. Galimberti, R., and Montanari, U. An algorithm for hidden line elimination. *Comm. ACM* **12**, 206, 1969.
21. Jones, C. B. A new approach to the hidden line problem. *Comp. J.* **14**, 232, 1971.
22. Loutrel, P. A solution to the hidden line problem for computer-drawn polyhedra. *IEEE Trans. Comp.* **C19**, 205, 1970.
23. Matsushita, Y. Hidden line elimination for a rotating object. *Comm. ACM* **15**, 245, 1972.
24. Bouknight, W. J. A procedure for the generation of 3-D half-toned computer graphics presentations. *Comm. ACM,* **13**, 527, Sept. 1970.
25. Gourad, H. Shading of curved surfaces. *IEEE Trans. Comp.* **C20**, 623, 1971.
26. Mahl, R. Visible surface algorithms for quadratic patches. *IEEE Trans. Comp.* **15**, 1, Jan. 1972.
27. Warnock, J. E. *A Hidden Surface Algorithm for Computer Generated Half-Tone Pictures.* TR 4-15, Department of Computer Science, University of Utah, 1969.
28. Watkins, G. S. *A Real-Time Visible Surface Algorithm.* UTECH-CSc-70-101 Department of Computer Science, University of Utah, June 1970.
29. Pitteway, M. L. V. Algorithm for drawing ellipses or hyperbolae with a digital plotter. *Comp. J.,* p. 282, Nov. 1967.
30. Smith, L. B. Drawing ellipses, hyperbolae, or parabolae with a fixed number of points, and a minimum inscribed area. *Comp. J.,* **14**, 81, Feb. 1971.

Systems Design and Interfacing

4.1. THE DESIGN PROCESS

Introduction

The preceding three chapters have discussed, in order, (i) the applications of, (ii) the hardware components used in, and (iii) the software tools available for inter-active computer graphics systems. These elements are usually pieced together to produce a *system* which can process one or more particular applications. In general, a system capable of processing the requirements of one application will not be suitable for another. Hence a certain amount of "tailoring" is necessary to produce a system suitable for a given application. It is this tailoring, or design process, which is the subject of this final chapter.

In most applications the main interest of the user of the system concerns the external appearance of the interconnected devices and the associated software, whereas the producer of the system is largely concerned with the internal hardware and software components. The latter is interested in the external characteristics only inasmuch as they complete a saleable product.

There are a variety of attitudes towards the design of systems, taking into account to a greater or lesser degree the requirements of the user and producer. At one extreme, the producer, who must spend large amounts of money to develop a new system, wishes to use existing configurations for all jobs and tries to fit a user's application to some available equipment. On the other hand, the user ideally requires an individually tailored system for each job he wishes to perform.

There is often a need for a mediator between these two conflicting interests—someone with a knowledge and appreciation of the difficulties encountered by both parties. We shall call this third party the designer, although in practice there is rarely just one. Sometimes design is achieved by negotiation between user and producer, the latter usually dictating most of the possibilities by virtue of his expertise in system production. A more common practice nowadays is for the user to hire a design consultant to look after his interests more effectively than he could do himself.

Some users may want to buy an existing system because it is cheaper than a tailor-made one, so their interests are already close to those of the producer. The user is the customer, and it is up to him to choose a method of buying the system that meets his requirements.

Examples of graphical applications illustrating typically required external characteristics, of interest to the user, were described in Chapter 1. The hardware and software components of graphical systems, of interest to the producer, were the subjects of Chapters 2 and 3, respectively. What steps are needed to produce a system, constructed of such components, which can process such applications?

In the design process the various components of a computer graphics system are selected according to the kind of application concerned (e.g., alphanumeric, geometric, etc.) and the user's requirements (e.g., quickly changing pictures, infrequent digitization of coordinates, continuous monitoring of geometric input, etc.), subject to the constraints of cost, availability, size, noise, etc. Activities within the design process that help to achieve this can be separated into four phases, as follows.

(i)   Specification of design objectives.
(ii) Systems design (choice of components).
(iii) Detailed design of components and interfaces.
(iv) Evaluation of system performance.

Normally these phases are processed consecutively, but the results of any one phase may require changes to previous decisions, implying the retracing of earlier steps. A flow diagram for the complete design process is shown in Fig. 4.1. This shows that there is plenty of scope for user interaction. It should be

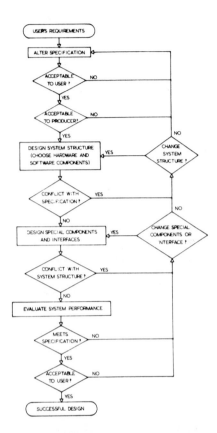

Figure 4.1. A flow diagram for the design process.

noted that it is possible to remain for indefinite periods of time in various redesign loops before a design is successfully completed.

The process is noticeably hierarchical, a factor which is common to human treatment of all complex matters. For example, we found it quite acceptable to describe the GT40 terminal at the end of Chapter 2 in more than one way. We introduced it in Fig. 2.10 as a system of fairly complex components. However, we later realized that it consisted of many other smaller units, such as the deflection drives of Fig. 2.11. The circuit designer is readily prepared to reduce other components of these subsystems to electronic- or logic-circuit representations such as Fig. 2.1 or 2.7.

During the design process, our attention is directed to different levels of complexity in an ordered sequence. We start off by looking at the user's requirements and produce a specification for the external characteristics of a system. In some respects we are defining the highest level of system complexity, which could be represented by the diagram of Fig. 4.2. After this we try to identify some system components which might produce these

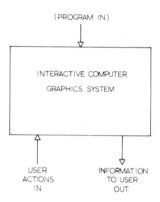

(PROGRAM IN)

INTERACTIVE COMPUTER
GRAPHICS SYSTEM

USER
ACTIONS
IN

INFORMATION
TO USER
OUT

Figure 4.2. A complete interactive computer graphics system.

external characteristics. For this we generate more detailed diagrams, such as Fig. 4.3. We then have to design any special components which cannot be obtained as ready-made units. We must also arrange any necessary programs or circuits to link the system components to one another and to the operator. These studies are highly detailed, and so, after completing them, it is necessary to move back up the hierarchy to check that the proposed system would, in fact, perform as the specification requires.

Of course, the phases of the design process are more complicated than the brief paragraph above indicates, and we must adopt a hierarchical method of description to discuss them further.

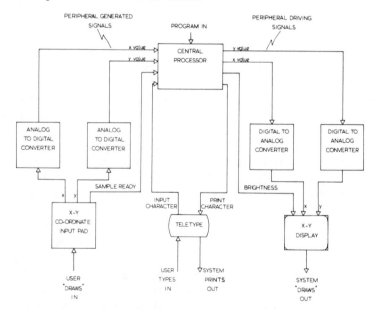

Figure 4.3. A simple interactive computer graphics system.

The Specification Phase

The first task in design is to define the structure which is to be produced. Hence a definition, or specification, of objectives must be obtained. At first sight it appears that the user is in the best position to provide this, but unfortunately few users have the experience necessary to express their needs accurately and unambiguously. Every manufacturer has his own "jargon" which is difficult for outsiders to understand, whilst most users tend to talk in terms of the application rather than the system. All too frequently the producer sells a system which does not do all that the user wanted, even though it meets the specified requirements. No foolproof method of obtaining a satisfactory (for either user or producer) specification exists. However, the more interaction between the parties, the more chance there is of success. This leads to the likelihood of alterations and additions to the specification as the other phases of the design process are performed, as shown in Fig. 4.1. It is essential that the design process be as flexible as possible, and that both user and producer keep an open mind about each other's problems.

The Systems Design Phase

When a specification has been decided, the designer must next select devices which could fulfil the particular requirements of the application. These devices may already be available, or they may have to be specially designed to suit unusual needs. This phase is often called *systems design*, although the same name could well be applied to the whole design process.

The end result of this phase is a description of the system structure, and the hardware and software devices to be used. A number of hardware graphical devices were described in Chapter 2. Software devices for manipulating graphical information were described in Chapter 3. The external characteristics of these devices are important at this stage.

It was pointed out at the beginning of Chapter 2 that an interactive computer graphics system can be considered as consisting of three major areas of operation: (i) the user program (including input processing); (ii) the display file; and (iii) the display processor.

The function of the *user program* is to manipulate potential pictures in symbolic form according to the application of the system. The manipulation might be inputting or forming new pictures by calculation, modifying existing pictures, swapping picture files from backing storage, or other high-level operations. Except in highly specialized systems, the user program is unlikely to be implemented in hardware. In most general-purpose systems the user program is a piece of high-level software operating in the mainframe computer system.

The user program must be able to access and alter the contents of the *display file,* which is an area of data storage (usually in the main computer store) containing a symbolic version of the picture or pictures to be displayed. The only other access to the display file is in read-only mode by the *display processor*, which implements the output of pictures. The activity of the display processor may be controlled by the user program (for example by a subroutine call, the display process discussed in Chapter 3), or it may be autonomous (i.e., the display processor continuously displays the contents of the display file, and the output picture changes as these contents are altered by the user program).

Since the display processor produces the final pictures, it must contain a section of hardware. Nowadays most display processors are, in fact, all hardware, but until quite recently software was used extensively. The reason for this was that although hardware offered advantages in speed and processor loading, it was expensive. The falling costs of hardware have influenced many areas of computer systems design in a similar way.

The function of the display processor is to convert the symbolic form of a picture stored in the display file into the corresponding pattern on the display screen. In some systems this may entail the use of an intermediate stage of storage of the picture, possibly in a form more closely resembling the actual display pattern than does the display file. The PICASSO system described in Chapter 2 gives an example of this technique.

Let us summarize the graphical system. Almost invariably in a modern system, the user program is high-level software, the display file is an area of computer store (sometimes permanently associated with the display processor), and the display processor is a hardware device which may be programmable (as is the GT40 terminal described at the end of Chapter 2).

A generalized schematic diagram of an interactive computer graphics system is shown in Fig. 4.4. It should be noted that this is in a different format to that of Fig. 4.3, even though it describes the same sort of system. The reason for this is that it describes the distribution of the control of activities within the system, rather than the distribution of the physical components. Such a diagram could contain more detail. Figure 4.5 shows details of the distribution of the control of activities in the system of Fig. 4.3. A diagram like this helps the designer to see how the software is employed in a system.

Multiple-terminal systems could be represented as parallel versions of Fig. 4.4, as shown in Fig. 4.6. However, this gives the erroneous impression that each terminal is entirely separate. Although the software in some systems may try to make the terminals look like this, the system designer is much more concerned with a realistic view of all the software involved and would prefer a diagram such as that of Fig. 4.7.

The difference between single- and multiple-terminal systems deserves some discussion here. The block labeled "executive" in Fig. 4.7 is responsible

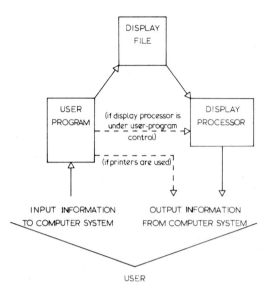

Figure 4.4. Generalized schematic diagram of a single-terminal interactive computer graphics system.

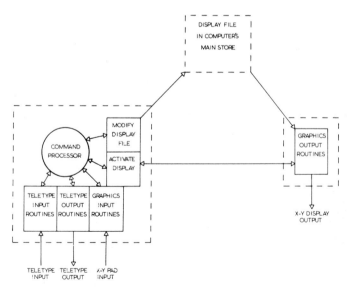

Figure 4.5. Control within a simple interactive computer graphics system.

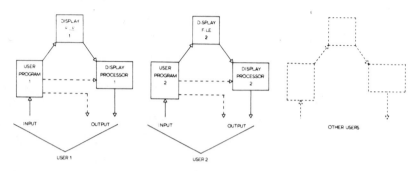

Figure 4.6. Generalized schematic diagram of a multiple-terminal inter-active computer graphics system.

for the sharing of time between all the terminals attached to the driving processor. In many systems another part of the executive also handles all input and output to and from peripherals. This means that for long periods of time the processor is "housekeeping", i.e., keeping track of data transfers, looking after peripheral interrupts, and swapping the active programs to and from the backing store. Hence it has reduced time available for processing user programs. Sometimes it spends so long housekeeping that it cannot give the user any time for several seconds.

We have already mentioned the human's response time in a graphical environment. The system designer's problems when designing a multiple-console system are more often concerned with the computer's response time. The important factors governing response times are many. It is easy to forget

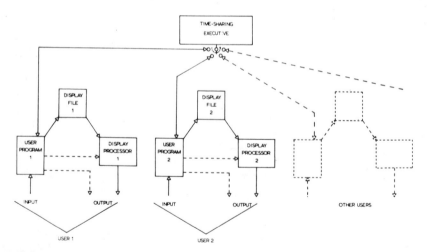

Figure 4.7. Multiple-terminal interactive computer graphics system showing the time-sharing arrangement.

one of them, thus rendering a system too slow to be used with the designed economical number of terminals in operation. The limiting factor is not usually hardware response times, but the time taken to perform the necessary software checks and actions which must be undertaken whenever an interrupt occurs. As will be indicated later, it is an impossible task to implement a multiple-terminal system without using interrupts.

The system designer's task is to propose a system which will achieve some given objective subject to a number of specified constraints. He might be required to produce a system which achieves a maximum part of the objective for a given fixed cost, or he might be asked to minimize the cost for a given system performance. These would be relatively simple constraints, and the job would merely require the choice of components whose external characteristics were as closely matched to one another and to the tasks to be performed as possible. However, frequently the design constraints do not give the designer as much freedom to choose components as he would like to have. For example, institutions will often want graphics facilities attached to their existing computer system, which might be unsuitable for the job. In addition, the money available to buy a system is rarely enough to implement a "good" design.

Bearing in mind the specified objectives and constraints, the system designer's next requirement is to have a memory file containing all information relating to manufactured components, prices and delivery, likely future technologies, programming techniques, etc. In short, he needs to know everything! His main task is to conjure up from this information systems which are likely to achieve the objectives specified. For this he needs to be infinitely creative!

In practice, these two ideals are unobtainable, and the problem appears to be in many respects more art than science. Usually the designer uses an intuitive "feeling" to discern the feasibility of possible solutions to a design problem, and eventually studies only a few of the most promising candidates in detail before selecting the final system.

The whole task of systems design is difficult because the field of choice is so wide. The designer's main tool must be a methodology by which he can attempt to reduce the field of choice without placing unwanted restrictions upon the structure of the system. This is a tool which must be provided by the designer himself, either as a natural ability or developed over time as his experience increases.

There are many ways of utilizing an information store to achieve some given objective within specified constraints. These methods do not guarantee optimum results, but they do cut down the total time involved in "goal-seeking." They are collectively known as *heuristics*, although it is tempting to describe them as "educated guesses." Research interest in the field of artificial intelligence (AI) has centered around the techniques of heuristic programming in mechanized problem solving for a number of years.

The following ideas are not to be treated as *the* method of achieving *the* design solution. They are intended as guidelines to a systematic approach to design problem solving, and they are certainly not the only steps by which systems synthesis can be achieved. The ideas introduced here are illustrated later in this chapter by a complete design example.

The systems design phase is the second of the four phases of design. The starting point for systems design is the specification. The form in which this is presented is important; otherwise the systems designer has to translate a lengthy statement of requirements into a concise and useful form. A good form of presentation is a numbered list of items which are to be considered in design, preferably split into two sections, one listing system requirements and the other listing design constraints.

The first job the systems designer performs is to convert these lists into some diagrammatic representation of the system, containing as much of the listed information as possible. A first diagram would be similar to Fig. 4.4 or Fig. 4.7, according to the number of terminals to be provided. This diagram shows the overall appearance of the system. The next step would be to generate a more detailed diagram, similar to Fig. 4.5. Both these diagrams are relatively easy to obtain; they merely involve the transfer of information from a written list (the specification) to a diagram.

The next step is not so straightforward. The two initial diagrams. showing mainly "soft" processes, must now be changed into a hardware systems diagram such as Fig. 4.3. The activities involved in this step are dependent on the kind of system being studied, and are best illustrated by examples. Accordingly, further details are provided in the design example later in this chapter.

Once a satisfactory hardware system configuration has been settled, the principal systems design task is complete. Attention is then transferred to details of component design and interfacing, which are discussed in the next section. At a later stage, the detailed system design must be evaluated, a task that is usually also performed by the systems designer. As we have already mentioned, an unfavorable evaluation may require a new systems synthesis phase.

The Component Design and Interfacing Phase

Many of the components chosen during the systems design phase are sure to be readily obtainable items. However, there may be the occasional need for special components which have to be built up from smaller units. During the third phase of the design process, these components must be fully considered and designed in an analogous manner to the complete system. Component design is a topic we cannot study further here, but many details are given in the references (1, 2).

The third phase of the design process also involves the physical interconnection of graphical devices to one another and to the central computer system driving the graphics. Usually the external characteristics of devices which are to be interconnected are not immediately compatible with one another. Hence it is necessary to introduce components which "match" them. These components constitute an *interface*. The external appearances (in electrical terms) of many graphical devices were described in Chapter 2. The designer must also consider the external characteristics of the central processor if he is to produce a reasonable design. Accordingly, this chapter contains a section describing the general characteristics of computers.

Interfaces are necessary where two incompatible channels have to communicate. These channels usually constitute the input or output to or from a device such as might be represented by a block in a system diagram. One example of an interface is a D-A converter, such as in Fig. 4.3, which converts the digital values output by the central processor into analog signals suitable for driving the input to the X-Y display unit. Other, less obvious, interfaces are often needed to convert digital signals into different digital forms. An example would be a TTL[1] output between 0 and +3 V which was to drive a corresponding MOS[2] input between 0 and −12 V. Some devices are themselves interfaces between electrical signals and audiovisual cues, or *vice versa*. The X-Y display unit is an example which converts analog voltages into an image suitable for human viewing.

Frequently, consideration of the details of interfacing will militate in favor of certain combinations of elements in a system design. The sort of factors which are important are the following: the voltage levels of the signals concerned, the power supplies required, the distances between devices, the number of devices to be driven by each driving element, etc.

Sometimes it is desirable to convert a signal into a different form at the output of the driving element and then reconstitute the original signal at the receiving element. This is particularly true where long distances intervene between two "adjacent" devices in a system. In this case economies are gained by transmitting the information in serial digital form, the principal advantages are that noise can be reduced and that only a few interconnecting wires are needed.

Another economical technique found in interface technology is that of *multiplexing*. This enables the same interface to be shared by different sets of

---

[1] TTL is a generic name for a family of electronic logic elements. It is a mnemonic referring to the method of construction. It stands for Transistor–Transistor Logic.

[2] MOS similarly stands for Metal–Oxide–Silicon logic.

devices. It finds most use where costs are to be reduced, or where large distances are to be covered between sets of devices. An example of the use of multiplexing is the Unibus system employed in the PDP 11 computer which drives the GT40 terminal described in Chapter 2. Telephone systems also employ multiplexing techniques liberally (for example, on "party lines").

Both of these economizing interface methods impose a reduction on the rate of transfer of information. Sometimes they introduce other problems, such as the use of a limited character code for values. Other forms of interface may be needed. Some could be achieved using software rather than hardware. Further information and details of interfacing techniques can be found in reference (3).

The interfacing and special component design phase requires detailed knowledge of electronic engineering, and is often undertaken by a specialist circuit or logic designer.

Evaluation of System Performance

This last phase of the design process is important in that it draws the designer's attention away from detailed matters, and ties up the loose ends which tend to be left hanging when too many different items have to be dealt with at once. The proposed system must be able to meet the original specification, otherwise one or more of the design phases will have to be retraced. Hence the kind of information that must be studied during this phase concerns the following: (i) the ability of the hardware and software to perform the specified tasks; (ii) the times taken by the hardware and software to perform the specified tasks—both interactive jobs and the rather more complicated background operations; and (iii) the satisfactory circumvention of constraints, particularly with regard to costs. Further details of the evaluation phases are shown in the design example later in this chapter.

In conclusion, we can see that the design process is complicated. It really needs to be studied by example. However, before an example can be studied, we need to recall some of the characteristics of central processing computers.

4.2. CHARACTERISTICS OF COMPUTERS

Introduction

An important subject in the design of interactive man–computer interfaces not yet studied in this book is the nature of the central processing system which drives the communicating peripherals. Accordingly, this section explores the form of central processing configurations and their links with the outside world. It will be appreciated that this topic is extensive. This section serves only as a general introduction to the subject, with emphasis on graphical applications.

For the devices that were studied in Chapter 2, the external characteristics were most important. The internal components were described to give an idea of the technologies involved, and the relative merits of each device in different applications. The central processors of computer systems are a separate class of device; their internal characteristics (in the shape of programs) assume as much importance as their physical connection to the outside world (the hardware interface). Chapter 3 was devoted to the description of graphical programs, and indicated how closely software is entwined with the hardware structure to produce the overall external characteristics of a computer.

Although there are many kinds of computer, and many ways in which programs can perform a given task, it is possible to describe some aspects of central processing systems in general terms.

Central Processing Configurations

Most central processing systems have several elements in common, e.g., the central processor, the main store, a backing store, a control console, etc., but these can be connected in many different ways, or *configurations*. In systems design, the configuration of the central processing system is important. The designer may be able to choose the configuration to his advantage, or he may be restricted to the use of a specified structure. In either case, he needs to understand the characteristics of the possible system structures.

The choice of central processors is large. The suitability of a processor is influenced by design criteria, but, at the same time, each processor generates its own particular requirements for other parts of the system. It is possible to identify several kinds of configuration which are commonly used as central processing systems for graphical applications. They can be graded roughly into three groups, according to their size.

Small Configurations. Applications which require little processing power, with only one user at a time, can use small central processing systems. In such applications, some inefficient operation of the processor and peripherals can often be tolerated, the most important design criterion being cost. Examples of applications which come into this category are computer monitoring of psychological "tracking" and "gaming" experiments, simple visual computer-aided design (CAD), "assembly" of pictorial data, simulation of simple real systems, etc.

The software for such systems is compact yet fairly complex, frequently written in assembly language or even machine code. The storage requirement must be reduced so as to minimize the hardware costs. A typical system is shown in Fig. 4.8. This comprises a processor with 8 k words (1 k = 1024), each 12 bits long, of main store, a teletype, and graphical input and output

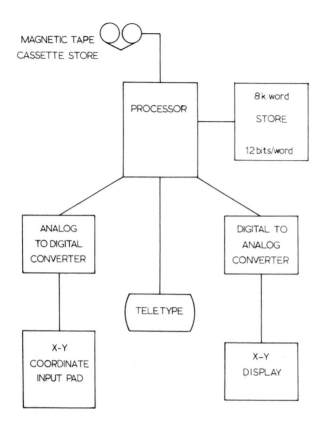

Figure 4.8. Typical small computer graphics configuration.

devices. The system could perform simple interactive CAD tasks as described in Chapter 1. Magnetic-cassette storage or high-speed paper tape may be used to store programs and data not currently in use. The complete system could cost as little as $20,000 (at early 1974 prices).

Many such systems exist and perform useful jobs in industrial laboratories and university teaching and research environments. Unfortunately the cost is still prohibitive for many other potential users. These small dedicated configurations are called *minicomputer* systems.

Medium Configurations. It is common practice nowadays to let more than one user have access to a central processor at a time, even with relatively small configurations. This enables a group of users to obtain a reduced capital cost *per user*. The applications remain much the same as for small configurations, but there is now more pressure to use the processor and peripherals with increased efficiency. Software and hardware requirements are both more complex; the former because it is usually desirable that different tasks can be performed for different terminals, using some time-sharing arrangement; the latter in order to provide more efficient control of peripherals, and to allow the use of a large backing store so that each user has as much storage space as he would have had with a minicomputer system.

A typical example of this kind of configuration is shown in Fig. 4.9. It comprises a processor with 32 k words, each 16 bits long, of main store, a magnetic-disc backing store containing 1024 k words (1 M word), a read-only memory loader (to retrieve system failures), and six interactive graphical terminals, each with a keyset, a display screen, a graphical input device, and a hard-copy photoreproducer. Such a system would cost in the order of $110,000, which means that the cost *per user* is about $18,000. (It should be noted that this is not a fair comparison with the single-user configuration described above, since the terminal is more sophisticated. A single-user system with the same terminal facilities would cost nearly $25,000.)

The cost comparison is favorable to the multi-access configuration, but the application must call for "clustered" terminals. In general, the more terminals that are served by one processor, the cheaper the cost per user. On the other hand, the response time per user will increase. Hence it is not possible to reduce the cost to an arbitrarily low value and still have a useful system.

Applications where such systems are used are typically in the teaching environment (usually in universities), or in small-scale stock control (where normally only textual information needs to be transferred) and similar

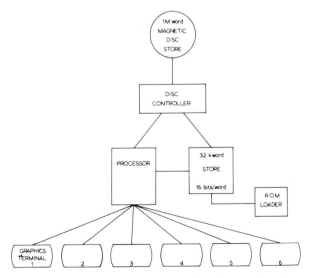

Figure 4.9. Typical medium-sized computer graphics configuration.

situations. These are rapidly expanding fields, and many new systems of this nature are currently being installed.

Large Configurations. Most applications using small or medium computer configurations do not require much processing power or data storage. However, applications for computer graphics systems do exist which have complex programming needs and require a sizeable data store. Typical examples of such applications are in the CAD of, for example, aircraft structures, motor-car bodies, bridges, buildings (to name a few complicated engineering problems), and in the simulation of atomic structures, plasma instabilities, seismic waves, gravitational collapse, and other predominantly visual phenomena associated with the theoretical sciences.

Systems capable of performing the calculations and managing the backing store necessary for these tasks are large and expensive. Such configurations have hitherto been restricted to non-interactive use. In simulation tasks in theoretical science interaction is usually not needed, but in engineering CAD it is essential. Hence, as CAD and similar applications have assumed greater importance, the number of large computer configurations with interactive terminals has increased dramatically.

A typical interactive computer graphics system of this size is shown in Fig. 4.10. It has 128 or even 256 k words, each of 24 bits, of main store, and more than 50 M words of fast-access back-up store. The element that distinguishes this system from a conventional large batch-processing configuration

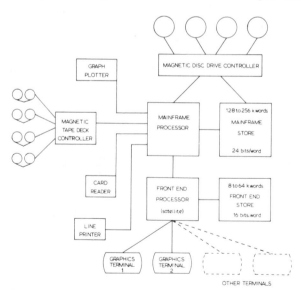

Figure 4.10. Typical large interactive computer graphics configuration.

is the smaller computer attached to the main processor. This is called a *front-end* or *satellite* computer. It can be used in several ways to control a number of interactive terminals.

One way of using the front-end processor is to control the transfer of information between the main processor and the terminals. Here the small computer would act as a programmed peripheral controller (see the following section on computer–peripheral communication). This arrangement is similar to the GT40 display processor–small computer link described in Chapter 2.

Another way of using the front-end processor is to let it operate autonomously for all small-scale tasks (acting as a medium configuration similar to that described above), but allowing it to pass complicated jobs to the main processor, receiving output information back at a later time and passing it on to the terminal. These are two extreme examples of the complexity of use to which the front-end processor can be put; other examples would place intermediate emphasis on the two processors.

The practice of front ending with small computers to obtain interactive access to a large configuration is widespread. It can be seen from Fig. 4.9 that this arrangement requires that graphical hardware be interfaced only to smaller computers. The elements that distinguish the system, from the user's point of view, from a smaller configuration are the hardware and software involved in the link between the two processors. This is an extensive and interesting topic in its own right, but one which unfortunately cannot be dealt with here [see (4)]. There is no need to restrict the configuration to one front-end processor; many non-graphical systems already use one mainframe processor linked by telephone lines to several satellites. Even larger and more complex systems can be constructed by interlinking more than one mainframe processor [e.g., the ARPA network in the USA (5)]. Eventually, such systems will undoubtedly be used to form extra large interactive graphical configurations.

Computer–Peripheral Communication

Although central processors vary in word length, store size, order codes, power supplies, logical voltage levels, etc., there is a surprising consistency in the form of communication with their peripherals. The needs of a communication system are two-fold: firstly, information has to be input from peripheral devices; secondly, information has to be output from the processor. Computer actions for the two possible forms of data transfer are summarized below.

(i) Data input:
  Ask peripheral for "read" data
  Wait until peripheral is "ready"
  Obtain data from peripheral

(ii) Data output:
Generate data for peripheral
Wait until peripheral is "ready"
Ask peripheral to "write" data

The order of these actions can in some cases be altered without affecting the transfer. The speed of the peripheral is an important factor which influences the order of actions, and also the device which controls the timing of the steps of the transfer. It is possible to allow either the processor or the peripheral to take command of the transfer at any time. There are three main methods which have been evolved to control peripheral activity. These fit a particular niche according to the speed of the peripheral concerned and the amount of money available. The choice of any one of these methods is determined by the design criteria; it then influences the nature of external systems and interfaces. The three communication methods are described below.

Link Activated by the Central Processor. In systems using this method of communication, *all* peripheral activities are under the control of the central processor. The arrangement of such a link is shown in Fig. 4.11. The processor sends out a signal to access the required peripheral. If the peripheral is not ready, then it tells the processor that it is busy. When it is ready, then the processor can ask it to transfer data in the appropriate direction. The advantages of such a technique are twofold: firstly, all peripheral actions are governed by software, making it easy to change the way in which transfers are achieved; secondly, the hardware interface is simple, and hence inexpensive. The disadvantage of the technique is that the timing of activities is in the hands of the programmer. Unless he is competent, one of two situations is liable to arise; either the processor will waste time waiting for peripherals to

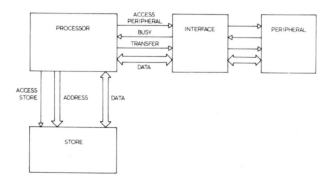

Figure 4.11. Processor-controlled peripheral activity.

become available, or the processor will spend too much time processing other jobs and keep the peripherals waiting longer than necessary. Hence, there is a high probability that either the processor, or the peripherals, or both will be used inefficiently. This may not be important in some applications where small computers are dedicated to a single task, but in other cases, especially multiple-terminal systems, it is essential to obtain maximum efficiency from all the devices in the system.

In order to overcome this problem, one of the two following techniques is usually adopted so that the peripheral can to some extent control the timing of transfer activities.

Link with Data Transfer by Interrupt. Here the processor initiates a peripheral activity, but does not have to ask later whether the activity has been completed. Instead, the peripheral *interrupts* whatever the processor is doing later at the moment the activity is finished. The processor then "remembers" what it was doing, whilst it decides whether a further action is required from that peripheral. At the same time, the processor can ask for data to be transferred in the appropriate direction. If further action is required, it can be instigated immediately so that the peripheral achieves near-perfect efficiency. The processor is only asked to stop processing other work when a decision is needed. The arrangement of this kind of link is shown in Fig. 4.12.

Usually a system of this kind transfers one computer word at a time. It is rather less flexible than the processor-activated link described above. It also requires more complicated interface hardware and is hence more expensive. However, it overcomes the timing disadvantages of the previous method in all cases except where the peripheral activities take such a short time to finish that the processor spends little time doing real work because it is being interrupted so frequently. A good example of a device which causes this kind

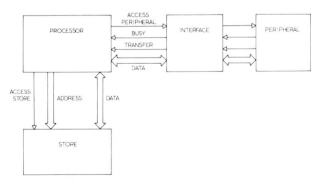

Figure 4.12. Peripheral activity using interrupt.

of problem is a magnetic data disc store. This snag is usually countered by allowing the peripheral to transfer "blocks" of information rather than words, and to transfer directly to and from the main computer store using direct memory access.

Link with Data Transfer by Direct Memory Access. In this system of communication, the central processor initiates the transfer of a block of information between the peripheral and the main computer store. Because the transfer involves more than one word of data, the processor needs to specify much more information to the interface than in the previous two systems. Since this information (which consists of values representing relevant store addresses, the number of words in the block, relevant peripheral addresses, etc.) must be stored by the interface, this becomes more than a characteristic-matching device, and it is usually referred to as a *peripheral controller.* The arrangement of this kind of link is shown in Fig. 4.13. The signals driving the peripheral are different to those from the processor, in contrast to the other two techniques. As was mentioned in the last section on computer configurations, it is possible for the peripheral controller to be a small computer itself. This has the advantage of great flexibility since we can use software to change the form of individual transfers. A new development is the *microcomputer*, a very small processor with little store, but operating quickly, which is ideally suited for the job of versatile peripheral controller (Digital Equipment Corporation, Maynard, Mass.: MPS Microprocessor Series Modules).

Often in this scheme the peripheral controller interrupts the processor when the transfer of the block is complete. Hence provision must be made for the interrupt hardware, and the total cost of such a communication system is high. However, this arrangement offers the most efficient use of both peripherals and processor, releasing the latter for more important work for the greatest possible time.

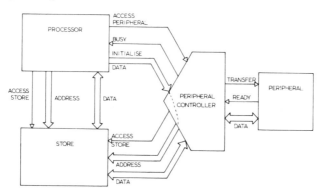

Figure 4.13. Peripheral activity using direct memory access.

4.3. DESIGN EXAMPLES

Introduction

One of the difficulties encountered in teaching design is that experience is such an important requirement for the student. Hence, although it is possible to discuss principles and methodologies of design in general terms, there is also a need for detailed study of particular examples, especially in an area where the design decisions can be made over such a wide range of techniques and equipment. It would be difficult to continue this discussion of systems design without seeing the results of applying some design criteria to at least one example. In order to avoid confusion an example has been chosen which is of the simplest type of configuration.

There is, unfortunately, insufficient space to detail any other examples here. This means that we cannot fully consider the implications of multiple-terminal interactive operation. This is a subject of much interest in the computing world at present and can be studied further in references (4) and (6). Another way of looking at systems design and a further systems design example can be found in Chapter 17 of reference (1).

A Small Interactive Computer Graphics System

This example is of a single-terminal minicomputer--based system, which represents the simplest configurations currently in use.

Specification. It will be assumed that the following statements adequately describe the required performance of the system to be designed.

(i) The interactive tasks to be performed involve both graphical and textual input and output. A trial task is specified in which the operator assembles electric-circuit diagrams on the display screen using a graphical input device, and assigns names and values to the electric components using a teletype keyboard.

(ii) All textual output from the computer will be in hard-copy form.

(iii) All textual input to the computer must be echoed in hard-copy form.

(iv) Graphical output should be in both hard- and soft-copy forms. Soft-copy display should occur at a sufficiently high speed to convince the operator that it is continuous. Soft-copy output should be on a large screen (10 in. X 8 in.).

(v) Graphical input should be echoed in soft-copy form conforming to (iv) above.

(vi) User programs can be developed using a different computer system (quite a common practice nowadays). They are to be written in an interactive high-level language such as BASIC or APL. (Language is not specified completely.) User programs will be relatively small (maximum of 200 high-level statements).

(vii) Only one operator can use the system at any time.

(viii) The primary design constraint is that the cost of the system must be minimal.

The above specification is far from comprehensive, but enough requirements are listed to notice that the more statements there are describing a system specification, the more restricted the choice of components becomes.

A complete specification is rarely obtained in practice, especially for complicated systems. In colloquial terminology "the bugs are never ironed out", and alterations are sometimes made years after a system has been installed. It is possible to view the specification of the design objectives as a continuous process which is intertwined with the design process itself. It reflects the difference between what the customer at first imagines he *should* be able to achieve, and what he eventually realizes he *will* be able to achieve.

Systems Design. Each designer has his own way of producing possible systems to satisfy the required objectives. It is desirable that this divergence of approach to synthesis problems should exist, and hence the precise steps to be taken in the design of this example will not be listed. The object of giving the example is so that the "feeling" of design decisions in a realistic situation can be communicated. Each design problem must be approached logically, and logical approach starts at the highest level. Hence the first task is to transfer as much information as possible from the specification to a system diagram. This has been attempted in Fig. 4.14.

The designer now has to determine the nature of each of the components to be chosen. In order to do this, he must call on his specialized knowledge.

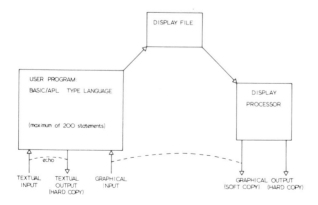

Figure 4.14. Small system design example: generalized diagram.

He knows that the principle objective is to minimize cost, and since the cheapest computers belong to the minicomputer families he is almost certain to choose one of these. The central processor with store is usually the most expensive item in a system of this size. It is important to choose a minicomputer which can achieve the specified software performance with a minimum of store. There is little to choose between a 12-bit word length and a 16-bit word length (the 12-bit word length is cheaper); most currently available minicomputers would need 8 k words of store to operate the size and kind of programs specified. It is important that any necessary operating software be (i) available from the minicomputer manufacturer and (ii) reliable. Hence if a particular language is specified, it should be ensured that that language has been used by other owners of similar computers and has been found to work satisfactorily. Too many system designs fail becuase insufficient care is taken when investigating the software background of particular computers.

A further consideration for store size is the size of the display file. The trial task specified would require an average of about 1000 to 2000 points on the display at any time. However, many of the points can be generated by display subroutines (hardware or software symbol generators) since elements in electric circuits are frequently repeated. If necessary, a vector generator would be helpful in reducing the time taken to display the pictures. This will be considered later. The main point at the moment is that the description of each picture (i.e., the display file) is unlikely to occupy more than 1 k word of store for the task described. Hence it can be accommodated within an 8k word store of one minicomputer or other. (It should be pointed out here that the choice of computer is beginning to narrow rapidly, and it is at this point that detailed knowledge of the capabilities of *all* minicomputers would be a useful asset. This depth of knowledge unfortunately takes a long time to build up. Usually the computer manufacturers themselves undertake designs of this kind, simply because they are the only people who can afford to employ full-time system designers. Naturally, the resultant designs are biased towards these manufacturers' own products.)

The final consideration determining store size concerns the likely future modifications to the system. Discussion with a customer will often elicit the previously unspoken wish to keep open the possibility of future expansion of his system. The foremost expansion to allow for is in store size. Thus it may be a good idea to choose a 16-bit word length which will allow for a direct expansion to 32 or 64 k words of main store.

A factor which may be important during the final checking of the design is the processor's speed of execution of instructions. Most minicomputers have similar speeds of operation, with store cycle times of about 1 μs. The effect of a slow speed of operation will be discussed later. A sensible choice of central processor and 8 k word store would cost about $7000.

Once the choice of a suitable processor and store has been made (it may be necessary to alter the choice later in the light of other design requirements), the interactive man–machine interface can be studied. A strict specification has limited completely the choice of textual communication, since the teletype is the only cheap device giving interactive textual input and hard-copy output. The teletype operates at a standard speed of 10 8-bit characters/s input and output (in fact 11 bits are transmitted for each character if start and stop bits are accounted for, giving a transmission rate of 110 baud). In most cases input and output are both asynchronous, and the teletype can be treated as two separate devices: firstly, an input keyset with a paper-tape reader; secondly, a character printer with a paper-tape punch. The current cost of a teletype is about $1700.

There are three sections of the system left to be determined: the graphical input, the soft-copy graphical output, and the hard-copy graphical output. Here again detailed knowledge of the available components is required and is just as difficult to obtain. One commercial unit which would fulfil all three requirements is the Tektronix 4010 storage display terminal, with a "joystick" tracker and a hard-copy photoreproducer (Tektronix Inc., Beaverton, Oregon: 4010 Graphics Terminal). For this unit the display processor would be partly software, probably written in machine code. Some computer manufacturers provide this kind of software, which would obviously influence the choice of processor (move back two paragraphs!). A system designed along these lines would appear as in Fig. 4.15. It must be noted, however, that the storage display terminal (which costs about $12,500) is more expensive than the central processor of the type of minicomputer that has so far been

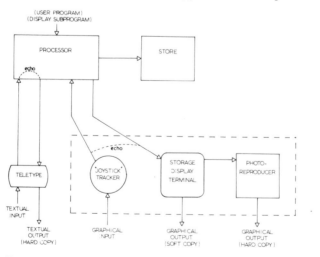

Figure 4.15. Small system design example: a possible implementation.

considered, and for this reason such a terminal would probably not be chosen. Another reason for not choosing this terminal is that is is designed for local soft-copy echo of textual input. This may be desirable in another system, but it is unacceptable for our specifications. It might be worth asking a customer if his needs are flexible enough to use this kind of terminal. Thus the specification could be adjusted to fit the design. Otherwise an alternative system must be derived.

A cheaper equivalent terminal is needed, possibly built up from separate components. One factor which helps the design is that a storage display (which is expensive) is not necessary and indeed could be disadvantageous for the tasks specified. The problems with the storage display are (i) the time taken to erase a picture and (ii) the fact that selective erasure of an area of a picture involves complete erasure followed by redrawing of the unaffected area. These difficulties were pointed out in Chapter 2, where it was also mentioned that continuously refreshed displays could circumvent the problem, since selective erasure involves simply removing the relevant item(s) from the display file. If a refreshed X-Y display is used, the digital signals from the computer must be converted to analog voltages (conversions which the complex terminal described above performs internally), thus increasing the cost. However, for the tasks specified, low precision is acceptable and the extra cost is relatively small. When the cheaper electromagnetic large-screen displays are used (as specified), the limiting time factor for the display of each part of a picture is the time taken to deflect the electron beam across the screen. This is typically 3 μs/cm or 60 μs for a full-screen deflection. The cost of digital-analog conversion and the display is about \$2500. Similar units based on television displays and a local store, for example the Computek 300 (Computer and Systems Engineering Ltd., Rickmansworth, Herts., UK: Computek 300 Graphics Terminal), cost more than twice as much. However, the software requirement would be less.

Graphical hard copy could be obtained from the cheaper display by switching the display output to an X-Y pen recorder, or a similar plotting device, which would be cheaper than a photoreproducer. The same digital-analog converters could be used, but the program timing would have to be altered since the deflection rate of an X-Y pen recorder is only about 1 ms/cm (a factor of 300 slower). Since hard-copy output does not have to deceive the eye of the operator, this is an acceptable arrangement. The necessary slowing down of the display program would have to be carefully designed for ease of operation *before* choosing a final central processor. The cost of a suitable X-Y pen recorder would be about \$750.

A less expensive graphical input device than the "joystick" tracker might also be available. Some units (such as the resistive pad) still require analog-digital conversion, but other devices (such as the sonic pad) perform their own conversion in a clever and cheap fashion. In order to conform with the specification, the input must change rapidly enough to appear continuous. Experience has shown that a suitable input rate is about 25 pairs of coordinates per second. It is possible to make a suitable low-precision unit for about $1500 (including conversion to digital form).

There are alternative graphical output devices which plot incrementally, avoiding the need for analog–digital conversion. These devices either produce hard copy and are expensive, or display soft copy on a television tube (e.g., the PICASSO system described in Chapter 2) and work too quickly for the computer to refresh them without using an intermediate store (which is also expensive). Information about all display devices, graphical hard-copy producers, and coordinate input devices is clearly another requirement for the computer graphics system designer.

A system constructed of the cheapest components described above is shown in Fig. 4.16. The total cost of this system would be about $15,000, as opposed to the system of Fig. 4.15, which would cost about $21,000.

At the present time the components of Fig. 4.16 probably constitute the cheapest possible system in terms of hardware. However, they present a significant software load to the central processor. In addition, the programs needed to operate such hardware must usually be purchased from the manufacturer of the computer. Hence, choosing the cheapest hardware components is not necessarily the way to produce the cheapest system. Again, the wider the designer's knowledge and experience, the more chance he has of reaching a satisfactory compromise between the objectives and constraints of

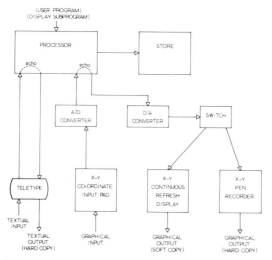

Figure 4.16. Small system design example: a less expensive implementation.

his design. The components for the design example above have been chosen as though the software is either free of charge or very cheap.

Interfacing. If the system of Fig. 4.16 is accepted as a reasonable configuration, then, according to the general scheme of the design process shown in Fig. 4.1, the next phase is to check the interfaces between the individual components of the system. (Special components have been deliberately avoided in this example.) In terms of electrical signals, there are five major interfaces to be considered. These are briefly discussed below.

Processor–Store Interface. This is a standard item provided by the minicomputer manufacturer to his recommended store. It needs no further consideration unless the designer contemplates using a non-standard store.

Processor–Teletype Interface. Again, for most minicomputers, this is a standard item, and needs little further consideration. There are several types of teletype and corresponding interface, but it is usually possible to choose a suitable pair as an option at no extra cost. A discussion of teletype and similar serial interfaces is included in Appendix 1.

Processor–X-Y Input Pad Interface. This is a more specialized interface which involves translation from analog to digital signals. The pad is designed to form a new pair of coordinates about once every 40 ms. In order that the processor does not have to spend this long waiting for the pad to sample the coordinates, it is advisable to use an interrupt system of communication. If the stylus is not positioned on the pad, the interrupts can be suppressed. Thus coordinates are only transmitted when the operator is using the input device.

The system is small and has only one terminal, so that it is unlikely that the terminal will need to be remote from the processor. Hence the need for serial transmission can be discounted. This also reduces costs, as long as the distance between devices is less than about 10 ft.

Possibly the "best" pad to use would be a sonic pad. This would produce two digital values (representing each of the coordinates) and a sampling (interrupt) pulse every 40 ms. The sampling pulse would interrupt the processor, which would then access the two values in turn. The complete system is shown in Fig. 4.17. The analog-to-digital conversion is achieved in the pad as described in Chapter 2.

Processor–X-Y Display and Processor–X-Y Pen Recorder Interfaces. These last two interfaces are closely related. In order to save components, the designer wishes to use one digital–analog converter for both devices, since only one of them will be used at a time. It has been mentioned that the pen recorder is much slower than the CRT display. If an interrupt system of communication were to be used, the device could time the transfers so that the processor would be unaware whether output was in soft- or hard-copy form. This would be advantageous from a software point of view. It

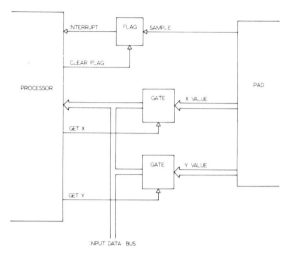

INPUT DATA BUS

Figure 4.17. Small system design example: processor–input pad interface.

would entail the provision of a feedback signal from the display and pen recorder to notify the computer that the electron beam or pen carriage had stopped moving. Such signals are available as options which increase the cost of the units by about $100 each. This is a worthwhile investment; the signal can also be used to generate a bright-up or pen-down signal.

Another point to be considered is whether each coordinate should have its own digital–analog converter, or whether one converter could be shared. This largely depends on the cost of the converter, which is in direct proportion to the accuracy required. Soft-copy accuracy is not critical, as has been discussed before; the hard-copy device suggested for this system is cheap and hence of low accuracy. There is thus no need for a highly accurate digital–analog converter, and a suitable unit is available at a cost of about $30. If a multiplexing arrangement were used in order to share a single converter between the two coordinates, the cost of the required electronics would probably exceed the cost of a second converter. Hence two separate converters will be used. The complete system is shown in Fig. 4.18.

The interfaces discussed above presented no major difficulties. In some cases they put constraints on the choice of devices. However, they did not require a redesign of the basic configuration. Certain possible problems were not mentioned. For example, the digital coordinate values from the input pad might be in Gray-coded binary, pure binary, or binary-coded decimal (BCD) form. The software may favor one or other of these formats. Another problem might arise if the digital–analog converter voltages are unsuitable for driving the display or pen recorder. Other similar problems may not be

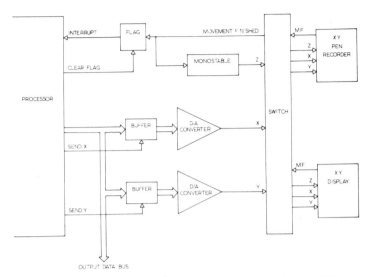

Figure 4.18. Small system design example: processor–graphical output interface.

discovered until the system is in use. Alternatively, they may be found in the final phase of the design process, in which the system performance is compared with the specification.

Evaluation. The evaluation phase requires a logical check of system capability *versus* application requirements. Hence, as a rough framework, the evaluation for this example will proceed in the order of the speciification statements at the beginning of this section.

(i) This statement concerns the overall performance of the system, and is best left until later.

(ii) The hardware is available; hence the software must direct all textual output to the teleprinter.

(iii) Again, software must arrange the echo of textual input.

(iv) The hardware is available; software must redisplay soft-copy pictures within 0.1 s to maintain a continuous image.

(v) Software must arrange the echo of graphical input.

(vi) The store size of 8 k words is large enough to hold the specified size of program. A minicomputer with a suitable language as standard has been chosen (the requirement for graphical manipulation will have narrowed the choice of processor considerably).

(vii) The hardware limits the number of operators to one.

(viii) The *hardware* costs are minimal. It is assumed that software is available cheaply.

Statement (i) must now be checked to ensure that software and hardware can operate quickly enough to maintain continuous images *and* hold interactive conversation with the operator. The evaluation consists mainly of adding up times involved in different software and hardware activities, and checking that complete image display can occur once every 0.1 s, whilst accommodating echo of graphic input every 40 ms and echo of textual input every 0.1 s. Because an interrupt system of peripheral communication is used, no time is wasted checking for busy devices. Hence there are no software "housekeeping" overheads. All the designer is interested in are the time to display a point, the number of points to be displayed, the time to echo a point, and the time to echo a character. These are approximately, in order, 60 μs maximum, 500 maximum, 100 μs, and 100 μs for a processor with a store cycle time of about 1 μs. If the store cycle time is longer, these times will be correspondingly longer. Taking the times given, the total processing time involved in 1 s, with a maximum picture and maximum input rates, is

points/image $\times$ time/point $\times$ refreshes/sec $+$ time/point echo $\times$ echoes/sec $+$ time/character echo $\times$ echoes/sec

$= (500 \times 60 \times 10 + 100 \times 25 + 100 \times 10) \ \mu$s

$= (300{,}000 + 2500 + 1000) \ \mu$s

$= 0.3035$ s.

This means that the processor spends 30% of its time looking after the peripherals. Computer engineers sometimes say that the processor is 30% *loaded*. The rest of the time it can process other work. This is probably satisfactory for this example. If required (for reduction in cost) the store cycle time could be three times greater. Alternatively, three times as many points could be displayed. If the loading were to be greater than 100% then the specification could not be met. In this case, the specification might have to be changed to allow the existing system to be accepted, or another configuration would have to be proposed and evaluated. It should be noted that modifications to the current proposal might allow a suitable reduction in loading. For example, in this design, if we had needed 2000 points, instead of 500, the loading would be 120%. However, this could be reduced by providing a hardware vector generator, if most of the 2000 points were in straight lines as would normally be the case. There are, of course, other factors which may be important. Unfortunately, there is too little space to discuss these further. Each application introduces its own idiosyncracies, which makes it difficult to generalize design procedures. As experience is gained, so the technique most likely to achieve results in any situation becomes more obvious.

As it stands, this design example has been successfully completed. It is to be hoped that it demonstrated some of the problems encountered in interactive computer graphics systems design, and some of the techniques for overcoming them.

4.4. CONCLUSIONS

This last chapter has attempted to link together the themes of the preceding sections. The design of systems to suit applications is an important subject. It has shown that hardware, software, applications, and users are interdependent entities. This creates a complex environment in which design decisions have to be made. There is never enough room to write all the relevant points about a subject as open-ended as interactive computer graphics. Where topics have been passed over quickly, we have tried to give more detailed references. The views we have expressed are our own interpretation of the subject. Other interpretations undoubtedly exist, and we would encourage continued divergence of viewpoint, especially where the design of systems is concerned. In final conclusion, we see a number of important concepts emerging from the consideration of interactive computer graphics that we have undertaken in this book. We postulate them as follows.

(i) There is already a wealth of applicable technology available to the computer graphics system designer. The problem of equipment design is no longer dependent on invention; rather, it depends on the proper choice and use of what is available, or likely to be available soon. The choice depends both on performance and cost considerations.

(ii) For all its power and possible sophistication, an interactive computer graphics system is no more than a high-performance input and output peripheral device. So long as the nature and structure of mainframe computers remains as it is, this will continue to be so. Perhaps, as the art of interactive computer graphics is developed, and its power becomes more widely appreciated, the design of the computer itself may be influenced by graphics, but this is still a futuristic concept.

(iii) The essence of interactive computer graphics system design lies primarily in the choice of the source problem to which graphical techniques are to be applied. Then the choice must be made of which part, or parts, of the problem can or will benefit from human interaction of various kinds. Finally the art of design must be exercised to interpret the chosen interaction so as best to fit the resources available. Clever interaction is possible with simple hardware and a minimal system, provided that the system and problem are well matched. If the system is to be asked to provide all things for all men, then it will certainly be costly and may well provide less to most men than a special-purpose less costly system could. A great deal of interactive computer graphics capability can be provided for little cost both in system overheads and system hardware.

REFERENCES

1. Newman, W. M., and Sproull, R. F. *Principles of Interactive Computer Graphics.* McGraw-Hill, New York, 1973.
2. Popplebaum, W. J. *Computer Hardware Theory,* Macmillan, London, 1972.
3. Cluley, J. C. *Computer Interfacing and On-line Operation.* Crane, Russak, New York, 1975.
4. Wilkes, M. V. *Time-Sharing Computer Systems,* 2nd edn. Macdonald, London, 1972.
5. Roberts, L. G., and Wessler, B. D. Computer network development to achieve resource sharing, *Proc. SJCC,* 1970, p. 543. AFIPS Press, Montvale, N. J.
6. Freedman, A. L., and Lees, R. A. *Design of Real-time Computer Systems.* Crane, Russak, New York, 1975.

Serial-Parallel Conversion: The Universal Asynchronous Receiver-Transmitter (UART)

Introduction

In many applications of interactive computer graphics it is not possible to have the working console close to the computer. It is often necessary, and almost always more convenient, to serialize the data for transfer between the computer and the graphics unit so that only one pair of wires is needed for the connection. This method of transfer has been adopted for the teletype because it was primarily intended as a telecommunications instrument. If a graphics unit is made to appear indistinguishable from a teletype (as far as the computer is concerned) then its connection to the computer can be a standard teletype interface.

The basic process of serial–parallel or parallel–serial conversion of data offers no difficulties. For the former, data can be entered serially into a shift register, and when this is full the outputs of the shift-register stages can be gated out simultaneously in parallel. Likewise, for the latter, a serial shift register can be loaded in parallel mode and the contents shifted out serially.

Such difficulties as do occur are principally due to the requirements of synchronization.

Naturally, several parallel channels can transfer more data per second than a single channel, so serialization imposes speed limitations. Most alphanumeric displays, such as VDU's, can be operated quite satisfactorily at teletype speeds, and the simpler and more economical devices conform to teletype standards, i.e., 110 baud or 110 pulse epochs per second. Where greater speed is required channels capable of operating at up to 2400 baud are common. There are faster channels for use in specially designed systems.

Since virtually every computer has an on-line teletype connection, most manufacturers, in the past, have had to design an interface to it conforming to the teletype and telecommunication system standards. The advent of MSI logic has now to a great extent precluded this necessity; there are now available single-chip microcircuits designed to perform the data conversions and synchronization necessary for the teletype interface, or for interfacing to modems attached to the telecommunication system. Such an element is likely to be a standard part of interactive computer graphics systems in the future. It is therefore appropriate to describe it briefly in this text.

THE UART

Figure A1 shows a schematic diagram of the device which consists primarily of two subunits, the *transmitter* and the *receiver*. The transmitter accepts eight parallel data bits together with five parallel control bits at logic voltage levels. After these have been set into the parallel register system, they are shifted to the parallel–serial transmitter shift register. They are then shifted out serially to a circuit capable of driving a relay or similar device which would operate a communication circuit.

There are a variety of "standard" modes of transmission and it is therefore necessary to adapt the UART for the system in which it will work. Provision is made by the manufacturer for various pin interconnections and preset terminal voltages which cause the device to conform to one standard or another. This is mainly achieved by encoding the control bits in the input register.

The receiver portion of the device is the complement of the transmitter. A serial register receives the transmission of a complete character. The bit format is checked before the whole pattern is transferred in parallel to the holding registers, whence, provided they are valid, the eight data bits can be strobed out at logic voltage levels. The correctness of the character is checked for parity (if required), for framing, and for overrun; the meaning of these last two expressions will be made clear in the following paragraphs.

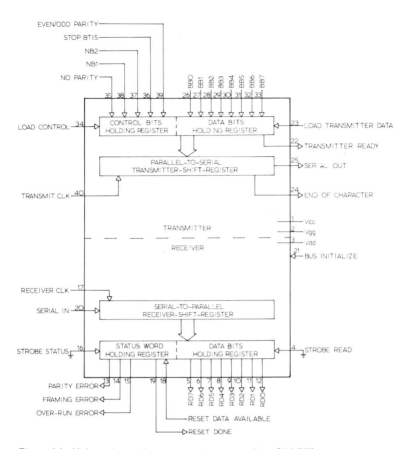

Figure A1. Universal asynchronous receiver–transmitter (UART).

The Synchronization Problem

The process of shifting serial data from register to register depends on the registers being synchronized to one another through the synchronization of their shift pulses. In computer systems this synchronization is ensured by a common clock. Over telecommunications channels a common clock is not available; some rough synchronization is available from the common 50 or 60 Hz electric mains but this is far from adequate. Instead the strategem of the "start/stop" principle is used. This requires that each device has a speed control tightly regulated to a standard figure. When a character is sent, both transmitter and receiver start virtually simultaneously, and transmit, or sample, at the rate governed by the speed control for the duration of one character.

Both devices then reset, starting together again when the next character is transmitted. Thus, provided the speed controls of the transmitting and receiving devices are within a few percent of the standard speed, the pulse epochs, as metered by each, will be no more than half a pulse out of synchronization with each other at the end of a train of 12 pulses.

In the case of the teletype or teleprinter, the speed control is generally vested in the drive motor which is driven from the a.c. mains, and is regulated to run at a fixed revolution rate. When a signal is transmitted, a "start bit" is sent which engages a clutch in both transmitter and receiver. The mechanisms of both machines then make one revolution virtually synchronized to each other. The clutches disengage at the end of the character, allowing both transmitter and receiver to reset ready for a new transfer.

In a computer interface there is no mechanism corresponding to that of the teletype. Hence a pulse metering system has to be devised by means of electronic logic. It is neither easy nor satisfactory to start and stop a stable oscillator arbitrarily to synchronize with incoming signals. Hence a crystal-controlled oscillation at a higher frequency than the transmission baud rate is generated and divided down for use. The UART is supplied with clock pulses at a frequency 16 times the baud rate, thus registering or counting 16 pulses per data pulse time. After a "start pulse" is detected the clock pulses are admitted to the timing counters. After eight pulses the input state is sampled, and thereafter at intervals of 16 pulses, corresponding to the midpoints of ideally received pulses.

The conventions governing serial transmission in telecommunications systems vary somewhat, but some features are standard. Briefly, the line state is maintained at high (logical 1 or "mark") while the line is idle. A character transmission commences with a "start bit" which is a logical 0 or "space". This is then followed, according to the system, by 5, 6, 7, or 8 data bits, and sometimes a parity bit, which can take logical value 0 or 1 depending on the code and the character. Again depending on the system standard, the transmission then terminates with 1, 1½, or 2 "stop bits" which are a logical 1 or "mark". The line then remains high (for idle) or goes low (for a new "start bit"). Because of the rigidity of the start and stop bit format, the receiver timing counter system can check synchronization. If this is outside the permitted variation a failure can be signaled.

The connection of the UART to a VDU or graphical processor is a simple exercise in logic design. It gives the advantage of making the VDU appear no different from a teletype, from the computer's point of view. A graphical processor, depending on its application, would generally require to work at one of the higher permitted data rates. The major advantage given to computer graphics by the UART will be that any graphical system can be directly and simply interfaced to any computer.

Index